HORRIBLE HISTORIES

THE HORRIBLY HUGE BOOK OF TERRIBLE TUDORS

Terry Deary & Neil Tonge   Illustrated by Martin Brown

SCHOLASTIC

Scholastic Children's Books
Euston House, 24 Eversholt Street
London, NW1 1DB

A division of Scholastic Ltd
London ~ New York ~ Toronto ~ Sydney ~ Auckland
Mexico City ~ New Delhi ~ Hong Kong

The Terrible Tudors
First published in the UK by Scholastic Ltd, 1993
Text copyright © Terry Deary and Neil Tonge, 1993
Illustrations copyright © Martin Brown, 1993.

The Terrifying Tudors
First published in the UK as Even More Terrible Tudors by Scholastic Ltd, 1998
Text copyright © Terry Deary, 1998
Illustrations copyright © Martin Brown, 1998

This compilation copyright © Scholastic Ltd, 2009

Some of the material in this book has previously been published in Horrible Histories:
Massive Millenium Quiz Book, The Terrible Tudors Sticker Book,
Terrible Tudors and Slimy Stuarts Quiz Book, Stratford-Upon-Avon and
Cruel Crime and Painful Punishment
Activities created and produced by The Complete Works,
St Mary's Road, Royal Leamington Spa, CV31 IJP.
Additional text by Dereen Taylor and Jenny Siklos.
Additional illustrations by Mike Phillips

All rights reserved

ISBN 978 1407 11090 5

Printed and bound by Tien Wah Press Pte. Ltd, Malaysia

2 4 6 8 10 9 7 5 3 1

The right of Terry Deary, Martin Brown and Mike Phillips to be identified as the author and
illustrators of this work respectively has been asserted by them in accordance with the Copyright,
Designs and Patents Act 1988.

CONTENTS

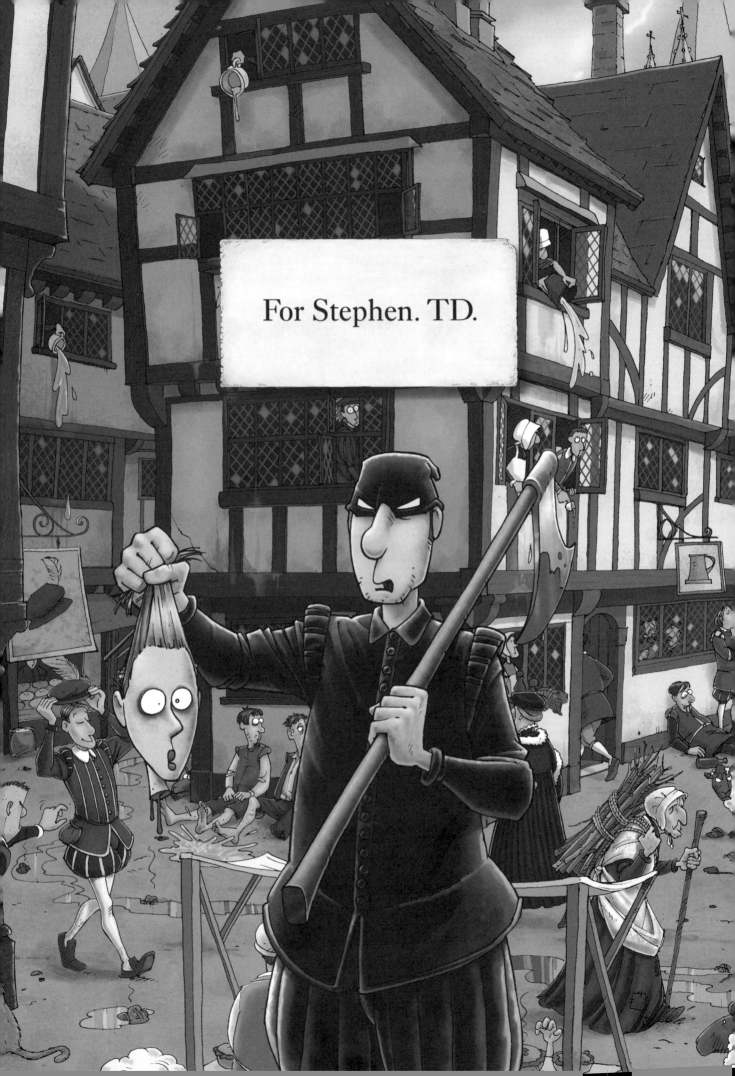

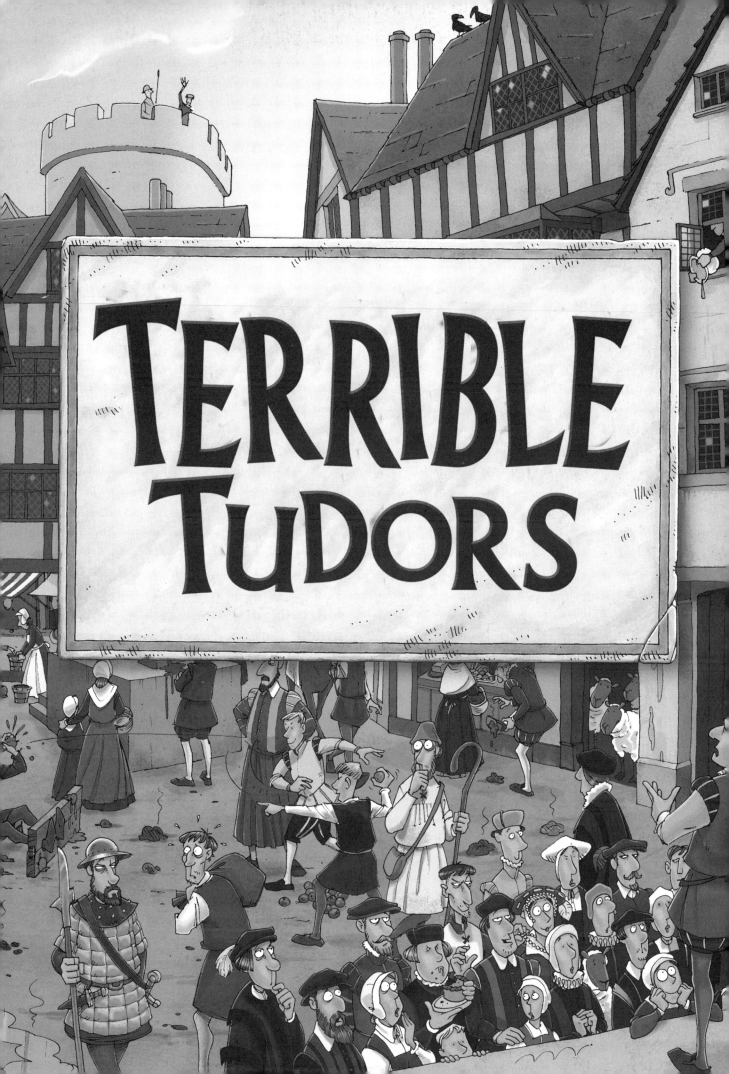

CONTENTS

Introduction

If you think history is horrible then this is the book for you!

Sometimes history lessons in school can be horribly boring…

Sometimes it can be horribly confusing…

And sometimes history can be **horribly** unfair…

But this book is about **really horrible** history. It's full of the sort of facts that teachers never bother to tell you. Not just the bits about the kings and the queens and the battles and the endless lists of dates - it's also about the ordinary people who lived in Tudor times. People like you and me. Commoners! (Well, I'm dead common, I don't know about you!)

And what made them laugh and cry, what made them suffer and die. **That's what this book will try to help you understand.** You might learn some things your teachers don't even know! (Believe it or not, **teachers do not know everything!**)

There are one or two activities you can try. That's about the best way to find out what it was like to be a common Tudor.

There are some stories that are as chilling as the chilliest horror stories in your library. (You may have to read them with the light turned off in case you are scared of the shadows!) The facts and the stories should amaze you and teach you and amuse you, and sometimes make you sad.

Hopefully you'll find them all **horribly interesting**.

The terrible Tudors

What is a terrible Tudor?

What your teacher will tell you...
The Tudors were a family who ruled England, and poked their noses into the rest of Great Britain, from 1485 till 1603. The grandfather was Henry VII, his son was Henry VIII and the grandchildren were Edward VI, Mary I and Elizabeth I.

Five rulers and 118 years that changed the lives of the English people.

Who's who?

HENRY VII

Henry VII (Henry Tudor of Lancaster) King from 1485 to 1509

Defeated King Richard III at the Battle of Bosworth and took his crown. Married Elizabeth of York to stop their two families whingeing scrapping over the crown.

Henry VIII King from 1509 to 1547

Son of Henry VII. Wanted a son to keep the Tudor line going and he didn't care how many wives he had till he got one.

HENRY VIII

When he got rid of his first wife by divorcing her, the head of the Catholic Church (the Pope) didn't approve of it ... so Henry made his own church (the Church of England), with himself as the head.

Henry got rid of the Catholic monasteries with their monks and nuns. (The money he got for their riches came in very handy!) But he still worshipped as a Catholic, and chopped off the heads of those who didn't.

~ HENRY VIII's WIVES ~

GOOD WIFE GUIDE

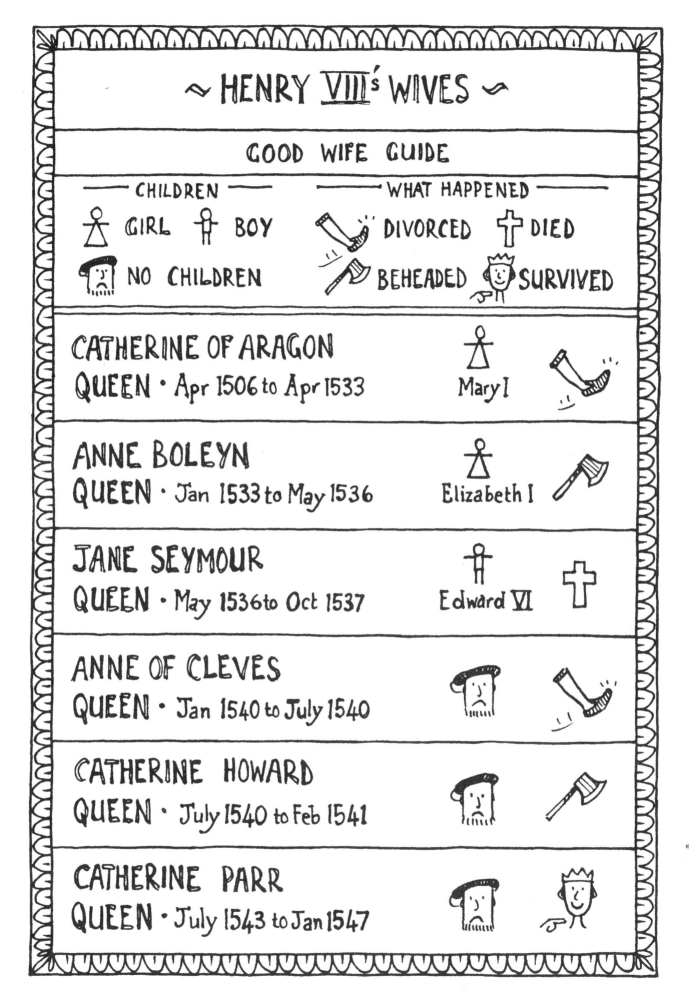

- CHILDREN -
- 👧 GIRL 👦 BOY
- NO CHILDREN

- WHAT HAPPENED -
- DIVORCED ✝ DIED
- BEHEADED SURVIVED

CATHERINE OF ARAGON
QUEEN · Apr 1506 to Apr 1533
Mary I

ANNE BOLEYN
QUEEN · Jan 1533 to May 1536
Elizabeth I

JANE SEYMOUR
QUEEN · May 1536 to Oct 1537
Edward VI

ANNE OF CLEVES
QUEEN · Jan 1540 to July 1540

CATHERINE HOWARD
QUEEN · July 1540 to Feb 1541

CATHERINE PARR
QUEEN · July 1543 to Jan 1547

Anne Boleyn's last words before she had her head chopped off were **not**, "I'll just go for a walk around the block!"

Edward became king first, even though he was the youngest. That's because a male child always took the throne before a female child. The same rule still applies in England.

EDWARD VI

Edward VI King of England from 1547 to 1553

Was too young to rule, so had a Protector, the Duke of Somerset, to "help" him out. King Edward was engaged to Mary Queen of Scots, but this fell through. Just as well, really, as Edward was a Protestant and Mary a Catholic, which would have caused big problems. The Duke of Northumberland, made Edward get rid of Somerset. Northumberland became the next Protector – what a surprise! Poor Edward was a sickly lad and died of tuberculosis at the age of 16.

Lady Jane Grey Queen of England in 1553

Put on the throne by Northumberland, who had persuaded Edward to make her his heir because she was a Protestant, and was great grand-daughter of Henry VII. She was also Northumberland's daughter-in-law! Lady Jane sat on the throne for nine days then Mary Tudor raised an army and walloped Northumberland. So Lady Jane was pushed off her throne and her head was pushed on the block.

LADY JANE GREY

Mary I (Mary Tudor) Queen of England 1553 to 1558

Was a devout Catholic, so she made the Pope head of the English church again. Married King Philip of Spain, also a Catholic. People were frightened of Philip's power, and the marriage led to Wyatt's rebellion, which was crushed by Mary's army. Philip, never short of an idea or two, persuaded Mary to fight the French. The English lost. Mary was getting

MARY I
(MARY TUDOR)

more unpopular by the minute, but was probably too insane to care. Ended up with the nickname 'Bloody Mary', owing to regular head-choppings and burnings of Protestants.

ELIZABETH I

Elizabeth I Queen of England from 1558 to 1603

Had pretended to be a Catholic while Mary Tudor was Queen, just to keep her happy. But changed both herself and England into Protestants when she came to the throne. Locked up Mary Queen of Scots and chopped off her head because she was a Catholic, and because Catholic Europe thought that Mary should be Queen of England. Elizabeth never married, because she said that she was married to England! But she had a definite soft spot for the Earl of Essex, which didn't stop her from having **his** head chopped off as well.

Terrible Tudor Limericks

Confused? You may be, but try learning these limericks, and you'll easily remember…

Henry VII
Henry Tudor beat Richard the Thirder
When the battle turned into pure murder.
Henry pinched Richard's crown
For the ride back to town.
He was top man! He could go no furder.

Henry VIII
King Henry was fat as a boar
He had six wives and still wanted more.
Anne and Kate said,
"By heck! He's a pain in the neck!"
As their heads landed smack on the floor.

Edward VI
At nine years the little King Eddie
Had a grip on the throne quite unsteady.
He was all skin and bone,
Grown men fought for his throne
And by sixteen young Eddie was deadie.

Mary I

Bloody Mary, they say, was quite mad.
And the nastiest taste that she had
Was for protestant burning
Seems she had a yearning
To kill even more than her dad.

Elizabeth I

A truly great queen was old Lizzie,
She went charging around being busy.
She thought herself beaut,
But her teeth looked like soot
And her hair it was all red and frizzy.

Terrible Tudor times

1485 – reign of Henry VII

Henry Tudor beat King Richard III at the Battle of Bosworth Field and became the first Tudor king. The Wars of the Roses ended – they had been dividing the country for over 30 years.

1487 A boy called Lambert Simnel claims to be king. His revolt fails. Is given a job in the palace kitchens!

1492 Christopher Columbus lands in America – the world is never the same again!

1497 Perkin Warbeck tries to take the English throne. Warbeck hanged in 1499. England settles down under Henry VII and becomes richer and more peaceful than in the past.

1509 – reign of Henry VIII

1516 Mary I born – daughter of Henry VIII's Catholic first wife, Catherine of Aragon.

1517 First real Protestant revolt against the Catholic Church begins in Germany.

1520 Henry VIII appears at the Field of the Cloth of Gold – a ceremonious meeting between Henry and Francis I of France.

1533 Elizabeth I born, daughter of Henry's second wife, Anne Boleyn.

1534 Henry takes over as head of the Church in England.

1535 Henry begins to execute Catholics who object to his Church takeover.

1536 Anne Boleyn, (Elizabeth I's mother) executed and Henry begins to close down monasteries. 1537 Edward VI born – but his mother dies shortly afterwards. Edward is always a weak child.

1547 – reign of Edward VI

1547 Edward VI just nine years old when he takes the throne.

The Duke of Somerset runs the country for the boy. His title is 'Protector'.

1549 Kett's rebellion in Norfolk against the new Protestant king.

1550 The Duke of Somerset executed and replaced by Duke of Northumberland as the new Protector.

1553 Edward is ill. He is persuaded to name Lady Jane Grey as the next Queen – this is partly to stop the Catholic Mary getting her hands on the throne … but the plan doesn't work. Young Ed dies.

1553 – reign of Mary I

Mary tries to return England to the Catholic faith. She has over 300 Protestants burned.

1556 Thomas Cranmer, Henry VIII and Edward VI's Protestant Archbishop of Canterbury, burned at the stake for opposing Mary.

1558 The English lose Calais (in France) to the French people. Mary unpopular for this and for her marriage to the Catholic Philip II of Spain. Luckily she dies before she is overthrown!

1558 – reign of Elizabeth I

1564 William Shakespeare born.
1567 Mary Queen of Scots thrown off her throne. She flees to England a year later.
1568 England and Spain begin to argue over control of the oceans.

1577 Francis Drake begins his voyage round the world - returns in 1580.
1587 Mary Queen of Scots executed.
1588 The Spanish Armada tries to invade England but is defeated.
1601 The Earl of Essex rebels against Elizabeth and is executed.

1603

End of Terrible Tudors - in come the Slimy Stuarts.

Kett's Rebellion

In Norfolk, 1549, the problem was too many sheep and too few jobs. The grumbles grew into a revolt. The revolting Norfolk men were led by the most revolting Robert Kett - a local landowner. But Robert's rebels grew hungry and weak. Edward VI sent the Earl of Warwick to deal with them. The Earl cut the rebels to pieces … but they weren't as cut up as Robert Kett might have been. He was sentenced to…

… be dragged to Tyburn, where he is to be hung and whilst still alive his entrails taken out and burned before him, his head cut off and his body cut into four pieces.

As it happened, Robert was taken to Norfolk Castle and hung in chains over the battlements.

Terrible Tudor life and death

Life begins at 40

Would **you** like to have lived in Tudor times? A 1980 school history book said ... *All in all the Elizabethan Age was an extremely exciting time to be alive.* But this is a *Horrible History* book. You make up your own mind about how "exciting" it was when you have the real facts. For example ... You probably know a lot of people who are 40 years old, or older. But would you have known as many in Tudor times?

Imagine that ten children were born on a particular day in a Tudor town. How many do you think would still be alive to celebrate their 40th birthdays?

a) 6   b) 9   c) 1   d) 4

Answer:

c) On average, only one person in ten lived to the age of 40. Many died in childhood – the first year was the most dangerous of your life.

Why were Tudor times so unhealthy? Perhaps these will help you understand...

Half a dozen filthy facts

1 Open sewers ran through the streets and carried diseases.
2 Toilets were little more than a hole in the ground outside the back door.

3 Water came from village pumps. These often took the water from a local river, and that river was full of the filth from the town.

4 Country people made their own medicines from herbs, or went to an "apothecary". People still use herbal cures today … but would you take one from a Tudor apothecary who didn't know the importance of washing their hands before handling your medicine?

5 A popular cure for illness was "blood-letting". Most people believed that too much blood made you ill. All you had to do was lose some and you'd feel better. Where could you go to lose some blood? The local barber. (He had a part-time job as a surgeon when he wasn't cutting hair!) Sometimes the barber would make a deep cut; other times a scratch was made, followed by a heated cup over the wound to "suck" the blood out.

6 Some doctors used slimy, blood-sucking creatures called leeches to suck blood out of the patient. (And some doctors today still use leeches to cure certain blood diseases!)

Doctor, doctor…!

If you were a doctor in Tudor times, what cures would you suggest for illnesses?

Here are ten illnesses - and ten Tudor cures. Match the cure to the illness…

1. HEADACHE

A. Shave the head and smear with the grease of a fox. Or, wash the head with the juice of beetles. Or, crush garlic rub it in the head and wash in vinegar

B. Pour on tobacco juice

C. Mix the herbs thyme campanula and hyssop (this one could work!)

2 BAD CHEST

3 RHEUMATISM

D. The gall of a hare and the grease of a fox. Warm the mixture and place in the ear.....

E. Swallow nine lice mixed with a little ale each morning for a week

F. Put the herb, rue on your windowsill.

4 GOUT (swollen foot)

5 DEAFNESS

6 BALDNESS

G. Boil a red-haired dog in oil, add worms, pigs marrow and herbs. Make a mixture and put it on the affected area ~

H. Drink mixture of lavender, bay, rue, roses, sage and marjoram. or press a hangman's rope to your head.

7 PLAGUE

SMALLPOX 8

I. Wear the skin of a donkey

J. Hang red curtains round the patient's bed - the red light is the cure

9 HEAD-LICE

JAUNDICE 'BAD LIVER' 10

Answers:
1=H 2=C 3=I 4=G 5=D 6=A 7=J 8=F 9=J 10=E

23

How did you do, Doctor? It wouldn't really matter if you got them all wrong. Most of them wouldn't have worked anyway!

Patient, patient…!

If you were sick in those extremely exciting Tudor times, which would you rather do?
Feel sick … or try one of these extremely exciting Tudor cures?

Ten cures you wouldn't want to try…

1 Swallow powdered human skull.

2 Eat live spiders (covered in butter to help them slide down a little easier). Swallowing young frogs was suggested as a cure for asthma.

3 Fustigation – the patient is given a good beating.

4 Throw a stone over your house – but the stone must first have killed a man, a wild boar or a she-bear.

OF COURSE IT'S BIG.. HAVE YOU EVER SEEN THE SIZE OF A SHE-BEAR?

5 Eat the scrapings from the skull of an executed criminal.

6 Eat bone-marrow mixed with sweat.

7 Sniff sneezing-powder to clear the head.

8 Have burning hot plasters placed on the body to raise blisters.

9 Mix the blood from a black cat's tail with cream, then drink it.

10 Place half a newly-killed pigeon on plague sores.

Nowadays we know that the dreadful plagues were carried by fleas. The Tudors didn't know about the disease they carried. Still, they weren't keen on fleas because they bit and made you itch. They had a cure you might like to try if you ever have them in your bedroom…

First, to gather all the fleas of thy chamber into one place, cover a staff with the grease of a fox or a hedgehog. Lay the staff in thy chamber and it shall gather all the fleas to it. Also, fill a dish with goat's blood and put it by the bed and all the fleas will come to it.

DON'T SLURP!

Fleas love to bite humans to get at their blood. They might well dash off to a whole dish of goat's blood!

25

Terrible Tudor schools

Parents, grandparents, teachers and other old fogeys... they all do it. They all talk about "The Good Old Days". Then they go on to talk about how terrible it was in school. They say things like… When I was a young lad/lass/goldfish just knee-high to a grasshopper/grass hut/grass skirt schools were schools. You kids have it easy these days. We used to get a caning/whipping/sweet if we as much as opened our mouth/eyes/door. We had 6/12/25 hours of homework every night and we were kept in detention/ prison/vinegar until we did it. They were the best days of our lives!"

If they think **their** schools were tough it's as well they didn't go to school in Tudor times. (Or maybe they did and they're lying when they tell you they're only 39.) If they had they would know that…

1 Most village children didn't go to school. A few might attend a "Dame" school run by a local dame (woman).

2 Children rarely had books. They may have had "Horn" books, though. These were pieces of wood the shape and size of a table-tennis bat. On one side was a printed page with the alphabet and perhaps, the Lord's Prayer. The other side was blank and could be used to practise writing.

'HORN' BOOK FOR SHORTSIGHTED PUPILS

3 Richer children could be sent away to school. At first, the monks in the monasteries ran most of the schools, known as choir schools. Henry VIII closed the monasteries because they were run by the Catholic Church. He started a new church, the Church of England, but he lost the schools in the process,

and was left with only a handful of grammar schools. He had to encourage new ones to be set up, but in fact only 20 more grammar schools were established during his reign. So much for education!

How does your school compare with a Tudor school? Check out these Tudor school rules and decide…

What to expect at school

Timetable

School lessons went on from dawn till sunset with a break for school dinners.

(If you lived a long way from school, you'd have to get up in the dark to allow time for walking. The roads were muddy, cold and dangerous on the short winter days.)

~ SCHOOL RULES ~

No scholar shall wear a dagger or any other weapon. They shall not bring to school any stick or bat, only their meat knife.

Manchester Grammar School 1528
It is ordered that for every oath or rude word spoken, in the school or elsewhere, the scholar shall have three strokes of the cane.

Oundle School 1566
Scholars shall not go to taverns or ale-houses and must not play unlawful games such as cards, dice or the like.

Hawkshead School 1585
Punishment for losing your school cap . . . a beating
Punishment for making fun of another pupil . . . a beating.

School swots

Working hard at school was not always popular with the upper-class parent.

One father said, *I'd rather see my son hanged than be a bookworm. It is a gentleman's life to hunt and to hawk. A gentleman should leave learning to clodhoppers.*

~ SCHOOL MEALS ~

Breakfast
Bread and butter and a little fruit

Lunch
Rye bread, salted meat and ale

Tea
Bread with dried fruit and nuts – fresh fruit in summer

Rules at meal times
1 Wear a cap to keep your hair out of your food.
2 Don't wipe your mouth with your hand or sleeve.
3 Don't let your sleeve drag in your food.
4 Don't lean on the table.
5 Don't pick your teeth with your pen-knife or your fork.

Punishment for breaking a rule . . . a beating.

WHERE'S MY CAP?

School teachers

Their job (in Westminster School at least) was to see that their pupils:

behave themselves properly in church and school as well as in games, that their faces and hands are washed, their heads combed, their hair and nails cut, their clothes and shoes kept clean so that no lice or dirt may infect themselves or their companions.

School punishments

Schoolmasters would often beat their pupils. Henry Peachum wrote,

I know one who in winter would, on a cold morning, whip his boys for no other reason than to warm himself up. Another beat them for swearing, and all the while he swore himself with horrible oaths.

But they weren't all so bad. The headmaster of Eton in 1531 was Nicholas Udall. He wrote the first English play that wasn't religious, and it was also the first comedy play.

School holidays

No long holidays. Schools would close for 16 days at Christmas and 12 days at Easter, but there were no summer holidays.

Lessons

A class might have as many as 60 pupils. Many hours were spent learning long passages from textbooks by heart. This not only kept them all quiet – it also saved having to buy books! Main subjects: Latin, Arithmetic, Divinity (Religious Study), English Literature.

School sports

A Shrove Tuesday custom was to take money to school, and with it the schoolmaster would buy a fighting cock. The master put a long string on the cock and tied it to a post. Boys would then take turns at throwing a stick at the cock. If a boy hit then the cock became his - if every boy hit then the cock belonged to the schoolmaster.

School equipment

Pupils had to write with quill pens made from feathers. These would have to be sharpened with a knife nearly every day. The small knife used was called a pen-knife - and we can still buy "penknives" today ... even if we don't sharpen our ballpoints with them.

If you'd really like to know what it was like to write with a quill pen then you could try making one.

You need

1. A strong feather - goose quill is best, but turkey or any other strong feather will do.

2. A pen-knife – if you haven't a pen-knife then a Stanley knife will be just as good.

3. Tweezers.

4. Ink.

And an adult to make sure you don't get chopped fingers on the table!

How to make it

1. Shorten the feather to about 20cm.

2. Strip off all the barbs (the feathery part) from the shaft.

(Yes, I know! In all the pictures you've seen the writers appear to be writing with feathers. They hardly ever did they only used the shaft and threw the rest away. Honest!)

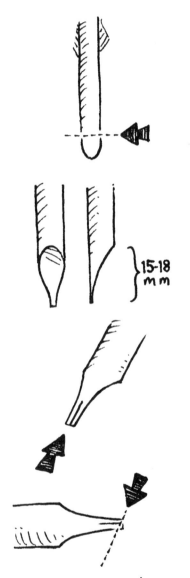

3 Cut the bottom of the shaft off with your pen-knife (Figure 1).

4 Shape the bottom of the shaft as in Figure 2. Take out the core with tweezers.

5 Make a slit at the end of the nib about 5mm long (Figure 3).

6 Trim the end of the shaft again, this time at an angle. (Figure 4 shows the angle for a right-handed writer)

7 Dip the quill in ink. Try writing an alphabet.

ABCDE ᴌ Gh 👁ᴊk l m

Test your teacher on Tudors

Here are a couple of facts your teacher (or parents or friends) may **think** they know. Perhaps you'll catch them out if you ask...

1 The first post

You: Please, Miss! (or Sir, or Fatface) Who had the first postal service in this country?

Teacher: I'm glad you asked me that...

(Teachers are always glad when you ask them something – it makes them think you are interested.)

...Of course, everybody knows that the famous Victorian, Rowland Hill, invented the postal service.

You: (with a sigh) But my book on the Terrible Tudors says the first postal service was invented in the reign of Elizabeth the First!

Then go on to quote these facts...

Rowland Hill created the Penny Post and postage stamps, not the postal service. Tudor Guilds and universities had private postal services. The government was worried about spies sending messages out of the country this way. So they insisted that a service under The Master of Posts should carry all letters sent outside England – that way they could read them if they suspected something!

2 A miss is as good as a mile

You: Please, Sir! (or Miss, or Fairy-features) If you asked Henry VIII how many yards there are in a mile, what would he say?

Teacher: I'm glad you asked me that... He would say 1,760 yards, of course.

You: That's not what my book on the Terrible Tudors says. It says that if you asked Henry VIII how many yards there are in a mile he would say, "It depends where you are."

Teacher: Eh!?!

You: (Explain) It wasn't till Queen Elizabeth's reign that a mile was fixed at 1,760 yards. Before that it depended on where you lived.

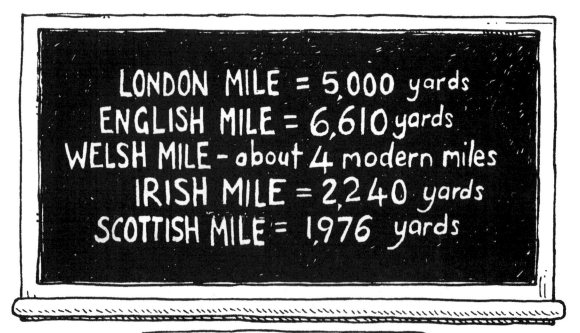

LONDON MILE = 5,000 yards
ENGLISH MILE = 6,610 yards
WELSH MILE - about 4 modern miles
IRISH MILE = 2,240 yards
SCOTTISH MILE = 1,976 yards

I THOUGHT YOU MIGHT HAVE KNOWN THAT, MISS!

Then count your lucky stars that you aren't in school in Tudor times!

Tudor crime ... and terrible punishments

In Britain in 1992 crime was the fourth largest "business" in the country – people on both sides of the law made 14 billion pounds. In Tudor times it must have been as bad, with more than 10,000 homeless beggars on the city streets. Many were simply rogues who tricked, cheated and stole from kindhearted people who thought they were helping the poor. Yes, there were more crimes in those days ... and more punishments. Some of them seem incredible today.

Thieving

Humphrey Lisle's story - Newcastle, 1528

Humphrey Lisle must have been worried. Dead worried.
He knew the English laws of 1528: steal up to eleven pence
and you went to prison. Steal twelve pence (one shilling) or
more … and you could be hanged. Humphrey had been one
of a gang of Scottish raiders who'd stolen much more than
twelve pence. One of the charges against Humphrey said that
he …

*at Gosforth, a mile from Newcastle, took prisoner twenty-seven
people passing by in the High Street, from whom he took 26
shillings and 8 pence. He ransomed all but seven whom he kept
for a while as slaves in Scotland.*

Stealing twenty-seven shillings! Kidnapping! Slavery!
Humphrey and the gang had been caught and locked up in
Newcastle jail. The gang were the worst villains in the North
and now they were safely in chains in prison.

They were still in chains when they went to court. One by
one the judge sentenced them to death. Humphrey's father
was sentenced to death first. Then it was Humphrey's turn.

"You admit to all the charges against you?" the judge
asked.

"Aye, sir," Humphrey answered.

"But I am not going to sentence you to death," the judge went
on.

A gasp of surprise went around the court. They had been
looking forward to seeing Humphrey's head stuck on a pole
on the town walls. It was just what he deserved, wasn't it? The
Newcastle people couldn't understand why the judge spared
Humphrey's life.

Can you give a reason for the judge sparing Humphrey s life? Was it because…

1 Humphrey had friends outside who threatened to have the judge killed?

2 Humphrey was very rich and offered the judge a lot of money?

3 Humphrey was the youngest in the gang and the judge wanted to give him a second chance?

4 Humphrey was Scottish and so was the judge?

Answer:

3. Humphrey Lisle was just twelve years old when he joined the gang that stole, burned, murdered and kidnapped its way through the north. The judge took pity on him. Within a few years Humphrey Lisle was working for the English … helping to catch Scottish raiders!

Believing is a crime

Tudor people were very concerned with religion. It was important to the kings and queens, to the people and to the law. Catholicism was the religion of England and most European countries until the 16th century.

But the invention of the printing press in the 15th century meant that more and more people had access to the Bible and were beginning to question the wisdom of priests. Ordinary folk were expected to believe all sorts of things, and were encouraged to buy "relics". These were things like bits of old bone and hair that some priests said belonged to saints. Yuk! Anyway, all this led to people wanting change within the Church.

And some kings and queens, who wanted absolute power without interference from Catholic leaders, were only too happy to encourage this change, which was known as the Reformation. The "reformists" were generally known as Protestants. There was a lot of hatred between the Catholics and the Protestants.

Catholics wanted…

The Pope as head of the church – services in Latin – churches decorated with paintings and statues.

Protestants wanted…

No Pope – services in English – plain churches.

Often, the hatred between them was terribly deadly…

Margaret Clitheroe's story – York, 1586

Margaret Clitheroe was a Catholic. In the days of Elizabeth I that was not a safe thing to be. But a lot of Catholics kept their religion and stayed secure by playing safe. They went to the Church of England services as the law said they had to. They kept their Catholic beliefs quietly to themselves.

But Margaret Clitheroe was not that sort of woman. She was a "recusant" - she refused to go to a protestant church.

Her husband, John, was a rich butcher in the city of York. "Margaret," he sighed, "the officers of the law cannot ignore you any longer. They will take you to court and fine you. Come to church with me today. It can't do you any harm!"

But Margaret was stubborn. "No, John." He shook his head and left for church. He walked by Micklegate Bar, one of the main gates of York. The remains of executed Catholics were still hanging there, more grisly than anything on his butcher's stall. He shuddered and wished his wife would learn some sense.

He'd have been still more worried had he known that Margaret was doing more than just missing church. She was also hiding Catholic priests in their house. But not for much longer.

The officers had started questioning people who knew Margaret Clitheroe. They were trying to make a case against her. When they captured a young servant, that case was complete. They threatened him with a beating, so he told them everything they wanted to know- and more. He told them about hiding Catholic priests. He showed them the hiding places.

On Monday 10 March 1586 they came for Margaret. She stood silent before Judge Clinch. "Have you anything to say, Margaret Clitheroe?" the judge asked.

Margaret said nothing. She knew that if she answered the charges then the law would call witnesses against her. The best witnesses would be her own children. If the children didn't want to talk then they would be tortured until they betrayed their mother.

The judge nodded. "Of course, the punishment for refusing to stand trial is Death By Crushing, do you know that, Mrs Clitheroe?"

Margaret knew. She had heard about "death by crushing". The accused was laid on the ground, face up. A sharp stone, about the size of a man's fist, was placed under the back. The face was covered with a handkerchief. A heavy door was laid on the accused. Large stones were placed on the door until the accused was crushed to death.

Margaret had to choose. Did she...

1 Remain silent and face death by crushing?

2 Stand trial and have her children as witnesses against her?

The good – the Justice of the Peace

Which would you rather do:

1 live by the laws of the Tudor land?

2 break the laws of Tudor times?

3 have the job of enforcing Tudor laws?

The people who had the job of enforcing the laws were usually Justices of the Peace. (We still have them today but they don't have so much power.)

If you were a Justice of the Peace you would have to…

1 stop riots

2 look after the building of roads, bridges, jails and poorhouses

3 decide how much local workers could be paid

4 report people who didn't go to church

5 be in charge of the whipping of beggars

6 check on the local alehouses.

But your main job would be to judge cases in your local court. Would you know all of the curious laws? Try to match the law to the crime first...

LAW

1 Archery

2 Unlawful games
3 Rescue

4 Barratry

5 Inmate
6 Riot

7 Recusance

8 Sedition

CRIME

A. More than 3 people making trouble together.

B. Quarrelling

C. Playing bowls, cards or dice on a holy day.

D. Stirring up trouble for the king or queen.

E. Refusing to go to church.

F. Not going to regular weapons practices.

G. Taking a person or an animal by force.

H. Letting part of your house to someone without a job.

Answers:
1 = F 2 = C 3 = G 4 = B 5 = H 6 = A 7 = E 8 = D

Now test your teacher! Bet they can't get more than 5!

Try your own court case

Now that you know the laws you can try a few cases. If you were a judge you'd have a lot of different punishments you could deal out. On the right is a list of the punishments - on the left is a list of crimes. Can you match the punishment to the crime?

41

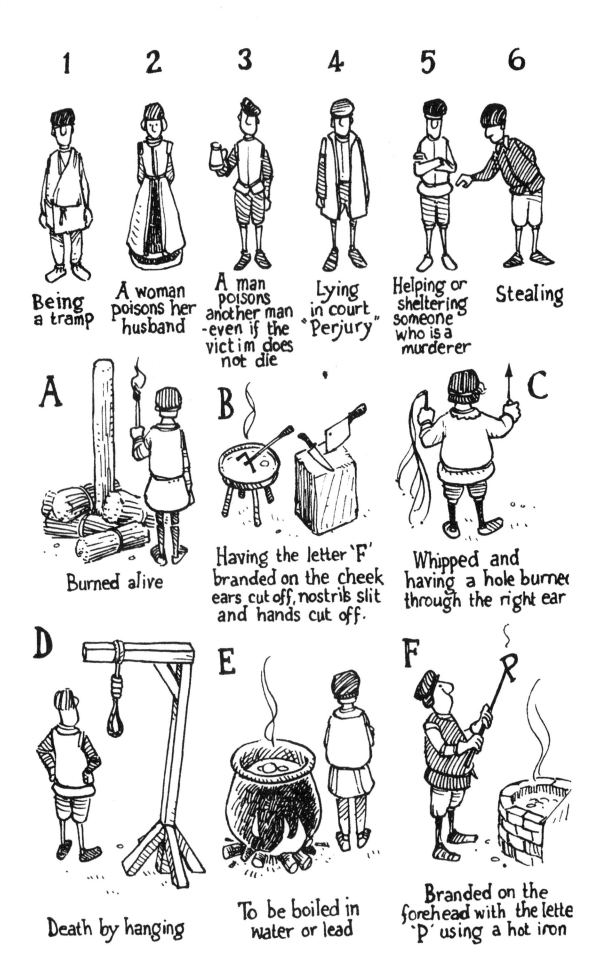

1 Being a tramp

2 A woman poisons her husband

3 A man poisons another man - even if the victim does not die

4 Lying in court "Perjury"

5 Helping or sheltering someone who is a murderer

6 Stealing

A Burned alive

B Having the letter 'F' branded on the cheek ears cut off, nostrils slit and hands cut off.

C Whipped and having a hole burned through the right ear

D Death by hanging

E To be boiled in water or lead

F Branded on the forehead with the letter 'P' using a hot iron

42

Rotten rules

There wasn't a lot of freedom in Tudor times. Henry VIII passed a law telling people how much money they could earn ... a craftsman could make just six pence a day in 1514. For that you had to work from five o'clock in the morning till six o'clock at night from March to September. In the winter months you would just(!) work from sunrise till sunset with one hour for breakfast and one-and-a-half hours for lunch. A servant could earn 160 pence a year – but a woman-servant could only earn 120 pence!

Elizabeth I passed a law telling people they could only wear clothes the queen thought suitable. And you had to wear a woollen hat on Sunday – or else! (That was so the English wool trade could make big profits and pay lots of lovely taxes to the queen!)

Even if you stayed out of trouble with the Justices of the Peace, you still had to worry about work. Most workers belonged to a Guild – a sort of union for their trade. There were guilds for goldsmiths and weavers and carpenters and shoemakers and so on. And every guild had its own laws. Heaven help you if you broke a guild law! It was worst for the young people who joined the guilds for the first time – the "Apprentices". Here are just a few of the rules they had to obey…

Apprentices must not use any music by night or day in the streets. Neither shall they wear their hair long, nor hair at their ears like ruffians (1603).

And the punishment for long hair? A basin was put over the boy's head and the hair chopped off in a straight line. He was then sent to prison for ten days! (We still call a straight-cut fringe a pudding-basin cut.)

ANY CHANCE OF TAKING THE PUDDING OUT FIRST NEXT TIME

Apprentices were in trouble in 1554 for *playing cards, drinking, dancing and embracing women,* and their appearance was so grand and flashy they were banned from wearing silk-lined clothes, from having beards or from carrying daggers.

In a Weaver's Guild meeting (1527) you had to behave or …
Any brother misbehaving at meetings to be fined six pounds of wax.
(Wax was valuable, as it was needed for candles)

…but worse, such was the hatred between the Scots and the English, that
Any brother calling another "Scot" to be fined six shillings and eight pence.
…that's twelve weeks' wages!

The Tudor law

The rich nobles had been a "law unto themselves" – the Tudors put a stop to that. They were no longer allowed to keep private armies.
Bribing of judges and juries had been common the Tudors stopped that … well, *mostly!*
The rich had been able to dodge the law – now rich lawbreakers could be taken before the Tudor kings' "Star Chamber". Punishments usually took the form of big fines.

Terrible Tudor detectives

The Tudors had no policemen. They did take it in turns to be "constables" and check on some of the laws. They also had local "detectives" called "cunning men", or "wizards". The village Cunning Man might use good magic to cure illnesses and tell fortunes. But he also had a use as a detective.

One of his methods of finding out a guilty person was to make a list of all the "suspects". Each suspect's name was written on a piece of paper. Each piece of paper was wrapped in a clay ball. The clay balls were dropped into a bucket of water. The one that unrolled first had the name of the guilty person on it! That's if the water didn't wash the ink off first!

The bad – the criminals

If you weren't afraid of being caught – or if you were very desperate for money and food to stay alive – you might become a criminal.

What sort would you like to be? A prigger of prancers? A dummerer? Or, maybe a ruffler?

What do you mean, you don't understand? If you're going to become a Tudor criminal you need to learn the language.

~ROGUES~ DICTIONARY

beak   **walking mort**

beak – magistrate
boozing ken – ale house
a bung – a purse
chats – gallows
a cony – an easy victim
cove – man
couch a hogshead –
   go to sleep
draw – pick a pocket
filchman – strong pole for
   walking or hitting
a foist – a pickpocket
glaziers – eyes
greenman's – fields

ken – house
lift – rob a shop
mort – woman
nab – head
peck – food
prancer – horse
prig – steal
a snap – a share of loot
stamps – legs
stow you – shut up
three trees with a ladder
   – gallows
walking mort – woman
   tramp

THAT HISTORY TEACHER'S A WALKING MORT. I WISH SHE'D STOW HER SO I CAN COUCH A HOGSHEAD. IN FACT IF YOU KEEP YOUR GLAZIERS ON HER I MAY JUST PRIG A NAP!

Become a terrible criminal!

Learn some of the language yourself – add new words of your own – and baffle everyone around you! Once you've grasped the language, you are almost ready to learn some tricks of the trade. But first you'll need a name – to protect your true identity. You need to change your name.

In Tudor times a few villains' nick-names were ...
Olli Compoli,
Dimber Damber,
Black Will,
Shagbag.
Women were ...
the White Ewe,
the Lamb, and so on.

What would you call yourself? You can make up your own name.

The Wickedness – the crimes

What villainy would you like to be involved in? You could try being one of these...

An Autem Mort – a woman who steals clothes off washing lines.

A Hooker (or Angler) – a thief who uses a long pole with a hook on the end to "lift" other people's property.

HOOKER
DUMMERER
I SAID CAN YOU PASS ME THE KNICKERS!
AUTEM MORT

They carry with them a staff five or six feet long, in which, within one inch of the top, is a little hole bored. In this hole they put an iron hook. With the same they will pluck unto them anything that they may reach. The hook, in the daytime, they hide and is never taken out until they come to the place where they do their stealing. They will lean upon their staff to hide the hole while they talk to you.

A Prigger of Prancers - a horse stealer.

A Ruffler - a beggar who tries to squeeze money out of you with a sad story about how he fought and was wounded in the wars.

A Dummerer - a beggar who tries to win sympathy by acting both deaf and dumb.

An Abram Man - a beggar who pretends to be mad, wears ragged clothes, dances around and talks nonsense… Try saying, "Please let me have some of your sheep's feathers to make a bed!"

Highway Robber - seems to be a beggar when he stops you on a quiet road, but when you take your purse out he snatches it and may throw you off your horse and take that too.

Palliard - a beggar with dreadful sores. Could be genuine disease, but (more often) they'd be faked.

They take crowfoot, spearwort and salt and lay them upon the part of the body they desire to make sore. The skin by this means being irritated, they first clasp to a linen cloth till it sticks fast. When the cloth is plucked off the raw flesh has rat poison thrown upon it to make it look ugly. They then cast over that a cloth which is always bloody and filthy. They do this so often that in the end they feel no pain, nor do they want to have it healed. They travel from fair to fair and from market to market. They are able to live by begging and sometimes have about them five or six pounds altogether.

A Doxy (or *walking Mort*) - a woman tramp.

On her back she carries a great pack in which she has all the things she steals. Her skill sometimes is to tell fortunes or to help cure the diseases of women and children. As she walks she knits and wears in her hat a needle with a thread in it. If any poultry be near she feeds them with bread on the hook and has the thread tied to the hook. The chicken, swallowing this, is choked and hidden under the cloak. Chickens, clothing or anything that is worth the catching comes into her net.

WOW! THEM'S GREAT SORES!

PALLIARD

CUTPURSE

IF I TELL YOU YOU'RE BEING ROBBED, WILL YOU LET ME GO?

DOXY

A Cutpurse – purses were small coin-bags hanging from the belt. If you couldn't "foist" the purse (dip in and pick the money out) then you would have to "nip" it (cut the purse off).

A good foist must have three qualities that a good surgeon should have and they are an eagle's eye (to spy out where the bung lies) a lady's hand (to be little and nimble) and a lion's heart.

Terrible Shakespeare

Terrible Shakespeare has been torturing school pupils for hundreds of years!

It isn't his fault, though. Teachers were taught by teachers who were taught by teachers who were taught, "Shakespeare is the greatest poet and playwright ever. You are going to listen to him even if it bores the knickers off you! Now, sit still and stop yawning!"

In fact, Shakespeare didn't write for school pupils to read his plays and study every last word. He wrote the plays to be **acted** and **enjoyed** … so act them and **enjoy** them.

You can start by practising a few Terrible Shakespeare insults. Go up to the nearest nasty teacher (or policeman or parent or priest) and try one of these insults on them. Then, just before they mince you into hamster food, say, "Oh, but Sir (or Miss or Constable or Your Holiness), I was just practising my Shakespeare. He's the greatest poet and playwright ever." Smile sweetly and add, "And you do want me to study Shakespeare, don't you?"

Here goes…

(Never mind what they mean … just enjoy saying them aloud!)
Feeling really brave now, are you? Then try…

Feeling suicidal? Then go up to the man with the biggest ears you can find and say Shakespeare's nastiest insult…

The Tudor Theatre

Being an actor in Tudor times was just a little different from today. For a start there were no actresses in Tudor theatre. All the women's parts were played by boys. Often the women in Shakespeare's plays disguised themselves as boys, so you'd have a boy pretending to be a woman pretending to be a boy. Nowadays women play the women's parts so you have women pretending to be boys pretending to be women pretending to be boys!

Get it? Oh, never mind.

Shakespeare's theatres were all open air stages. The audience would sit around three sides of the stage – if you were poor you would have to stand … and Shakespeare's play, Hamlet, went on for over three hours!

His plays are often performed on Elizabethan style stages today. You can see them in Shakespeare's birthplace, Stratford-upon-Avon.

Most of the audience couldn't read so it was no use putting up posters. The signal that a play was going to start was a cannon fired from the top of the theatre roof. Unfortunately, one such cannon shot set fire to the thatched roof of one of Shakespeare's theatres and burned it to the ground.

Dramatic facts about William Shakespeare

1 Shakespeare was born on St. George's Day (23 April) in 1564. He died in 1616… on 23 April, St. George's day! That must have put a bit of a damper on his 52nd birthday party.

2 Shakespeare chose the epitaph for his own gravestone. It says…

Some people think there may be new and priceless Shakespeare plays buried in the tomb … but no one has risked the curse of digging it up.

3 In his will he left his wife his *second-best bed, with the furniture.*

4 Some people have tried to rewrite Shakespeare's plays. In the eighteenth century, a man called Nahum Tate rewrote many. He took the sad and gory tragedies (like *Macbeth*) and gave them happy endings just because people prefer them!

5 Actors are very superstitious people. Their greatest superstition is that *Macbeth* is an unlucky play. Never, never say a line from the play (unless you are acting, it of course). Don't even say the title … call it "The Scottish Play" if you have to call it anything. And if you do act in it then watch out

… the "Macbeth Curse" may get you. This is the terrible bad luck that seems to happen to every production accident, illness and even death. Many actors will swear that it's true because it's happened to someone they know.

6 The most dramatic fact of all? Perhaps William Shakespeare didn't write William Shakespeare's plays! Some very serious teachers believe that the man called Shakespeare could not have written plays. Why not? Because…

a William Shakespeare's father could not read or write, nor could Shakespeare's children

b the few signatures of Shakespeare that remain show a very poor scrawl

c William Shakespeare was known in Stratford as a businessman, not a writer

d there are no manuscripts of Shakespeare's plays in the man's own handwriting – there are lots from other writers of the time

e he left no manuscripts in his will and no copies of his plays are mentioned as being in his house

f a monument put up in Stratford church 15 years after he died show his hands resting on a sack (a sign of a tradesman) not a pen

g there is no evidence, apart from the name, to link the Stratford actor/businessman with the playwright.

7 Professor Calvin Hoffman has studied the language used by writers. If you look at the way a writer uses words of a certain number of letters then you can recognise his writing. Every writer is different – just as everyone has different fingerprints. Yet Shakespeare's writing "fingerprint" is identical to that of another leading Elizabethan playwright, Christopher Marlowe.

So, did Marlowe write the plays and put William Shakespeare's name on them? Is it possible? No. Because, six months before Shakespeare's first publication, Christopher Marlowe is said to have been murdered.

Or was he…

Terrible Tudor mystery

The murder of Christopher Marlowe?

The murderer's story

Date: Wednesday 30 May 1593
Place: Eleanor Bull's Tavern, Deptford, London

Mrs Bull mopped at the spilt ale on the table with a dirty cloth. It dribbled onto the sawdust on the floor. Suddenly, three men clattered down the stairs and fell into the room. Three of the men she'd let the upstairs room to.

"Mrs Bull! Oh, Mrs Bull!" the skinny Ingram Frizer gasped as he clutched at his head.

"What's wrong?" the woman snapped. Frizer was a well-known trickster who'd tried to cheat her more than once.

The man took his hand away from his head. It was soaked in blood. "Murder!" he said hoarsely.

"Sit down," she said briskly. Frizer's two friends, Skeres and Poley, helped him to a bench. The woman mopped at the head wounds with her ale cloth and sniffed. "Not murder, Mr Frizer, just a couple of two inch cuts. You'll not die. Who did it?"

"Marlowe," the man moaned, "Christopher Marlowe."

The woman looked at the stairs and snatched a bread knife from the bar. "Roaming around stabbing people, is he?"

The wounded man shook his head slowly. "Not any more, he's not."

Mrs Bull relaxed. "You overpowered him, then?"

Frizer's voice dropped to a whisper. "I killed him!"

The landlady grabbed the man by the collar and marched him towards the stairs. "Let's have a look at poor Mr Marlowe, shall we?" she demanded. Frizer couldn't argue. Skeres and Poley lurked behind as she threw open the door.

The body lay on the floor. One lifeless eye stared at the ceiling. The other was covered in blood from a neat wound just above it.

"I knew you were trouble, you three," the woman moaned. "That Mr Marlowe seemed such a nice young man. What happened?" She looked closely at the body and shook her head. "Doesn't look a bad enough wound to kill a man that quick," she muttered.

Frizer swayed and let himself fall onto the bed.

"He was lying here, on this bed. We had our backs to him, didn't we Poley?"

Poley nodded. The local men said Poley made his money from spying. "Our backs to him," he said.

"Suddenly he jumped up from the bed, snatched my dagger and started stabbing at my head!" Frizer groaned. "I had Skeres on one side of me and Poley on the other. I couldn't get out of the way, could I?"

"He couldn't!" Skeres agreed. Everybody knew that Skeres was a cutpurse and a robber.

"If he attacked you from behind he could have killed you easily, not just scratched your scalp, Mr Frizer," the landlady argued.

"I moved," the man said lamely.

"Then he stabbed himself in the eye, did he?" Mrs Bull asked with a sneer.

"No!" Poley cried. "I managed to get the dagger from him. We struggled. It went into his eye by accident."

"A strange sort of accident. Doesn't look the sort of wound you'd get from a scuffle. Looks more like he was lying on his back when the knife went in," the woman said carefully.

The three men looked at each other nervously.

"Just one of those things," Poley mumbled.

"So what were you arguing about?" the landlady asked. "I didn't hear any argument."

"About the bill," Frizer said quickly.

"And why didn't your two friends help?" she asked suspiciously.

"It wasn't our argument," Skeres shrugged.

"You'll hang for this, Mr Frizer," Mrs Bull said contentedly.

Frizer looked up slowly from the bed. A curious smile came over his face. "Oh no I won't, Mrs Bull. Oh, no I won't."

And he didn't.

A strange sort of accident indeed. But the jury decided that was just what it was. You might have decided the same if you'd been on the jury. But looking back over 400 years you have a few more facts to go on. Here they are...

The powerful and important Sir Thomas Walsingham was a friend of all of the men and could have helped them get away with a plan such as this. Christopher Marlowe was certainly his closest friend.

Marlowe was in deep trouble at the time of his "death". His friend, Thomas Kyd, had just been arrested for having writings which said that Jesus was not the Son of God. The punishment for this was death. Kyd said the writings belonged to Christopher Marlowe! (It did Kyd no good being "put to torture" in prison a year late.

Frizer went back to work for Walsingham after he had been tried for the murder of Marlowe.

So what happened in Mrs Bull's tavern that day? If you don't believe Frizer's story, here are two other stories that fit the facts…

The execution theory

Marlowe had been careless. He'd left those writings in Kyd's room. Marlowe would be arrested and executed. Marlowe was as good as dead.

Kyd had accused Marlowe. But if Marlowe went to court he might have brought Sir Thomas Walsingham into all this. That would never have done.

Sir Thomas called his three loyal cut-throats to him. He gave them their orders, "Kill Marlowe and I will reward you well. Make it look like an accident and I'll use all my power to make sure the court lets you go free."

The three agreed to meet Marlowe in the tavern. As the playwright lay drunk on the bed, Skeres and Poley held him down while Frizer pushed the knife into his eye. Skeres or Poley then gave Frizer a couple of cuts on the head to back up their story of a fight.

Or…

The escape theory

Sir Thomas Walsingham was a great friend of Christopher Marlowe. He heard that Marlowe was about to be arrested for a crime that could lead to his execution. Sir Thomas wanted to protect his friend.

He called the four men to his house and told them of his plan. Marlowe must leave the country as soon as possible. As soon as he was safe abroad the other three must take a stranger to Mrs Bull's tavern and kill him.

After the murder, Frizer must confess. Say it was a fight and that "Marlowe" had been killed. When a man owns up to murder, the constables are interested in establishing the killer – not the identity of the victim. The stranger was buried in a grave named "Christopher Marlowe" and the real Marlowe was safe.

Of course, the real Marlowe was a successful playwright. Imagine Marlowe wants to go on writing plays. So he does. He sends them to Walsingham. Walsingham gives them to an actor. An ambitious young man who happily signs his own name to Marlowe's plays.

He signs them, "William Shakespeare".
Possible? What do you think? Remember, history is not always simple or straightforward. In cases like this historians make up their own minds from the facts that they have. So, you can be an historical "police officer". In cases like this, what you think is as good as what another historian might think.

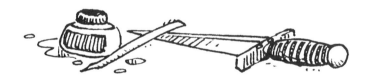

Terrible Tudor kings and queens

Things they try to teach you

Henry VII

Henry Tudor became King Henry VII after defeating Richard III at the Battle of Bosworth Field.

True, but Henry had a lot of help from other lords, including one (Stanley) who might have fought for Richard. When he chose to fight for Henry he won the battle for him and changed the course of English history!

Richard III was a grotesque man - he was hunch-backed and cruel.

Richard was no crueller than most rulers of the time. The stories of his twisted body were added to by Henry Tudor's history writers. England was full of cruel lords - only the cruellest of all could hope to control them and that was Henry Tudor!

Richard III died in battle crying, 'A horse, A horse! My kingdom for a horse!'

That's extremely unlikely! The lines were written by William Shakespeare 100 years after the battle in his play *Richard III*.

When Richard was killed in the Battle of Bosworth, his crown was found hanging from a thorn-bush and Henry was handed it on the battlefield.

It's a nice image, but not necessarily true.

Henry was fighting Richard III in the so-called 'Wars of the Roses'. Richard was fighting under the White Rose of the York Family emblem and Henry Tudor under the Red Rose of the Lancaster Family emblem.

In fact Richard fought under the banner of a Boar, while Henry Tudor battled under the Dragon symbol of his native Wales. The white-rose/red-rose idea was thought up by Henry Tudor years later.

 Henry VII was a clever man and a wise ruler.

True – but he was also a man of the Middle Ages with some strange ideas. The story goes that he'd heard that the Mastiff type of dog was the only one brave enough to attack a lion. But the symbol on the English flag was a lion – so he ordered all the Mastiff dogs in England to be destroyed! (Richard was just as superstitious. Freak weather conditions meant that there appeared to be two suns shining in the sky before the battle of Bosworth Field. Richard took this as a sign that he was going to lose . . . and he did.)

 Henry VII made England a wealthy country by carefully handling its money.

True – but Henry was so careful with money most people would call him very, very mean! And he wanted lots of money so that he didn't have to beg Parliament for it – which meant that he didn't have to take any notice of what Parliament said.

 All the money Henry VII saved for England was spent by his son, Henry VIII...

True!

Things you could try to teach them!

Henry VIII

• Henry is famous for his six wives. But, did you know that in just one year (1536) his first wife (Catherine) died, his second (Anne Boleyn) was beheaded and he married his third (Jane Seymour).

• Henry was fond of cock-fighting so he had his own cock-fighting pit built at Whitehall in London. There are different battles fought on the site today – it is number 10 Downing Street, the home of the Prime Minister!

•Henry was famous for his love of music. He composed many pieces and was a keen singer. He owned ten trombones, 14 trumpets, five bagpipes, 76 recorders and 78 flutes. It is said he composed the tune, *Greensleeves*.

• Henry was a show-off. He organised a great tournament near Calais in France, known as the *Field of the Cloth of Gold*. It seemed mainly a chance for him to display his own sporting talents. He is said to have tired out six horses while performing a thousand jumps . . . *to the delight of everyone.*

• Henry was an expert archer. He used to have competitions with a hundred of his guards and often did well. At the *Field of the Cloth of Gold* in 1520 he amazed people by hitting the bulls-eye repeatedly at a distance of 220 metres.

• Henry fancied himself as a wrestler. At a wrestling contest at the *Field of the Cloth of Gold* he created a stir by challenging King Francis I of France with the words. . . Brother we will wrestle. Francis couldn't refuse even though Henry was taller and heavier. Francis used a French-style trip and won – the English thought this was cheating; the French probably thought it served big Henry right.

• Henry liked to play an indoor tennis game called "Paume". He didn't go to see his wife, Anne Boleyn, executed. He was playing tennis while she had her head chopped off. As soon as he was brought the news of Anne's death, he rushed off to see his next love, Jane Seymour.

I'M BEING TREATED IN A VERY BACKHAND MANNER

• Even hard Henry VIII had a heart. He needed a son to carry on the Tudor royal name. He was so furious when Anne Boleyn produced baby Elizabeth that he refused to go to the christening!
• Henry wanted to get rid of Anne Boleyn for giving him only a female child. Her other babies died. One of the things he accused her of was being a witch. He had some support from the Tudor people in this. Anne had been born with a sign of the devil on her … she had six fingers on her left hand!
• Only his third wife, Jane Seymour, gave him the son he wanted – then she died a few days later. Of his six wives it was Jane Seymour he asked to be buried next to when he died.

• Henry agreed to marry Anne of Cleves after he was shown a picture of her. She turned out to be a bit uglier than the picture. Henry was so upset he accused the Dutch of sending him a horse instead of a princess. He called her the Flanders Mare and divorced her after just six months.

Elizabeth I - what they said about her

It's difficult to know what Elizabeth looked like because although there are a lot of portraits of her, she didn't pose for many of them. And if a picture displeased her then she would have it destroyed.

Many painters have done portraits of the queen but none has sufficiently shown her looks or charms. Therefore her majesty commands all manner of persons to stop doing portraits of her until a clever painter has finished one which all other painters can copy. Her majesty, in the meantime, forbids the showing of any portraits which are ugly until they are improved.
Lord Cecil

So, will we ever know exactly what she looked like? Only from what people wrote about her. Could you draw her from the descriptions?

She is now about twenty-one years old; her figure and face are very handsome; she has such an air of dignified majesty that no one could ever doubt that she is a queen.

VENETIAN AMBASSADOR

She is now twenty-three years old; although her face is comely rather than handsome, she is tall and well-formed, with a good skin, although swarthy; she has fine eyes and, above all, a beautiful hand with which she makes display.

ANOTHER VENETIAN AMBASSADOR

70

> *Her hair was more reddish than yellow, curled naturally in appearance.*

SCOTTISH AMBASSADOR 1564

> *In her sixty-fifth year her face is oblong, fair, but wrinkled; her eyes small, yet black and pleasant; her nose a little hooked; her teeth black (a fault the English seem to suffer from because of their great use of sugar); she wore false hair, and that red; her hands were small, her fingers long and her height neither tall nor short; her air was stately, her manner of speaking mild and good-natured.*

GERMAN VISITOR 1598

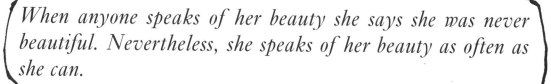

> *When anyone speaks of her beauty she says she was never beautiful. Nevertheless, she speaks of her beauty as often as she can.*

de MAISSE FRENCH VISITOR 1597

Elizabeth did not want to have her rotten teeth removed. Perhaps she was afraid. To show her how easy and painless it was, the brave Bishop of London had one of his own teeth taken out while she watched.

What Elizabeth I said about herself

I know I have the body of a weak and feeble woman, but I have the heart and stomach of a king, and a king of England too. I think foul scorn that any prince of Europe shall dare to invade the borders of my realm.

SHE WOULDN'T WANT THE STOMACH OF HENRY VIII

Her speech to her troops as the Spanish Armada approached
A weak and feeble woman? That's not what writers of her time said. Elizabeth had a temper which everyone feared. William Davison, her unfortunate secretary, was just one who suffered:
She punched and kicked him and told him to get out of her sight.
And…
She threw a slipper at Walsingham (her secretary) and hit him in the face, which is not an unusual thing for her to do as she is always behaving in such a rude manner as this.
And…
Once she sent a letter to the Earl of Essex which was so fierce that he fainted. He became so swelled up that all the buttons on his doublet broke away as though they had been cut with a knife.

What can we do about Mary?

In 1568 Mary Queen of Scots had to leave Scotland in a great hurry. She was suspected of being mixed up in the murder of her husband, and she was a Catholic. She also had a claim to the throne of England. She was a threat to Elizabeth, so what could Elizabeth do?

Elizabeth kept Mary in prison for a few years while she made up her mind. (It was 16 years in all Elizabeth could sometimes take a long time to make up her mind!) Then, in 1587, Mary was proved to be plotting against Elizabeth. The English Queen had to act quickly. If you were Elizabeth I what would you do? You could...

1 help poor Mary to get her Scottish throne back: after all she is related to you through Henry VII – but this would upset the Scottish Protestants and may cause a war with Scotland if the plan failed.

2 let her go abroad to Catholic France or Spain - but Mary might get those countries to join her in a war to take the English throne. The English Catholics would certainly support her.

3 hand Mary back to the Scots for trial and possible execution - but Mary is a relative.

4 execute her - but English Catholics might rebel with help from Spain and France. And could you be so cruel as to do this to a woman who came to you for help?

5 sign an order for Mary to be executed. Wait for the execution to be carried out, then try to cancel the order. When the cancellation arrives too late say, "Oh, dear! I did sign the execution order - but I never really meant it to be delivered!

It's the messenger's fault! Put him in the Tower of London!"
But nobody would swallow that, and Spain or France may
still attack.

6 keep Mary in prison – but English, French or Spanish
Catholics may try to free her.

What did Elizabeth decide? Number 5.

*The Queen's mind was greatly troubled. She signed a death
warrant for Mary and gave it to Davison, her secretary. The
next day she changed her mind but it was too late. The warrant
was delivered and Mary was executed. William Davison was
fined heavily and put in the Tower of London.*

According to one account, Mary was beheaded by a clumsy
executioner who took at least three blows of the axe and a bit
of sawing to finish the job. This eyewitness described it …

*The executioners desired her to forgive them for her death. She
answered, "I forgive you with all my heart for now, I hope, you
shall make an end to all my troubles."*

Kneeling down upon a cushion, without any fear of death, she spoke a psalm. Then she laid down her head, putting her chin on the block. Lying very still on the block she suffered two strokes with the axe, making very little noise or none at all. And so the executioner cut off her head, sawing one little gristle. He then lifted up her head to the view of all the assembly and cried, "God save the Queen!"

Elizabeth did apologise to Mary's son, James …

My dearest brother, I want you to know the huge grief I feel for something which I did not want to happen and that I am innocent in the matter.

So that was all right!

But the Spanish didn't believe in Elizabeth's innocence - they didn't want to. King Philip II of Spain was sick of English ships raiding his own, laden with treasure from his overseas territories. Philip was a Catholic, like Mary. So he used her execution as an excuse to send a huge invasion fleet, The Armada, to take revenge for these English crimes. But that's another story …

Mary's Secret Message

Did Mary Queen of Scots deserve to die? Elizabeth had sheltered her when she fled from Scotland. How did she repay Elizabeth? By plotting with Elizabeth's enemies, especially English Catholics, to kill her. Of course Mary didn't go shouting it from the rooftops. It was a secret plot between her and the English conspirators. The leader of these treacherous plotters was a rich young Derbyshire man called Anthony Babbington.

So, if it was secret, how did Elizabeth find out about it? She found out because she had a very clever spy in her service,

Sir Francis Walsingham. First, Walsingham sent servants to Mary's prison who pretended to work for Mary … in fact they were spying on her.

Every time Mary sent a letter to Babbington the servants took it to Walsingham first. Mary tried writing in code. But she had sent the code to Babbington first. Walsingham had a copy. This is Mary's code…

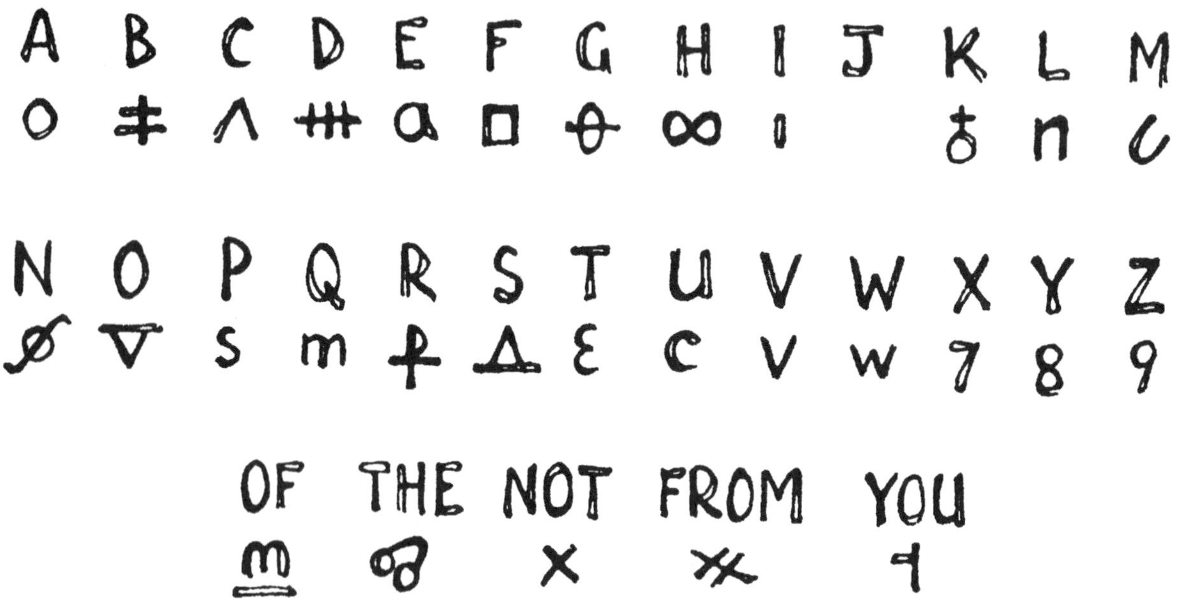

A	B	C	D	E	F	G	H	I	J	K	L	M
O	‡	∧	⧣	α	□	θ	∞	ı		δ	�885	ς

N	O	P	Q	R	S	T	U	V	W	X	Y	Z
ø	∇	s	m	ϯ	Δ	ε	ς	ν	w	7	8	9

OF	THE	NOT	FROM	YOU
m (underlined)	oȣ	X	⋊	٩

And this is part of the message that Walsingham read and passed on to Queen Elizabeth – the part that led to Mary's execution. Use the code to read it.

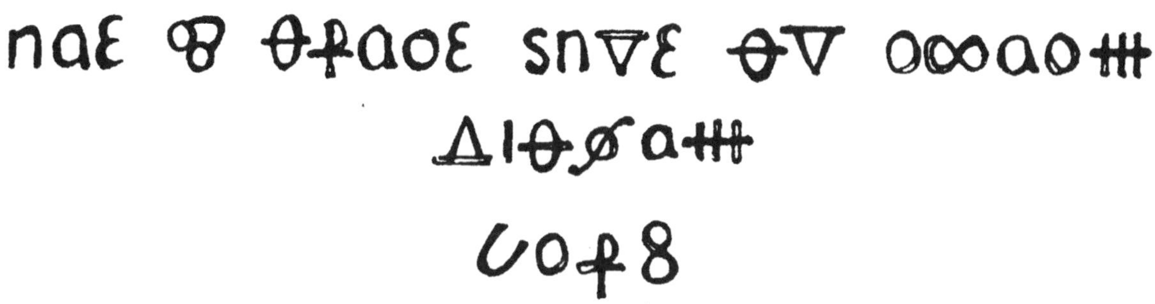

ηαε ⱷ θϯαοε sη∇ε θ∇ ο∞∞αο⧣

Δıθøα⧣

ςοϯ8

76

You could try writing your own messages in this code.

Elizabeth I's sharp and cruel tongue

It was said that if someone tall disagreed with her she would promise …

I will make you shorter by a head.

She seemed to have a thing about height. She asked a Scot how tall Mary Queen of Scots was. The man replied that Mary was taller than Elizabeth. Elizabeth said … *She is too tall, then; for I myself am neither too tall nor too short.* And, of course, Elizabeth then went on to make Mary Queen of Scots "shorter by a head"!

Elizabeth also made her favourite the Earl of Essex "shorter by a head" when he tried to lead a rebellion against her in February 1601. She was so fond of him that she wore his ring for the rest of her life. It must have upset her to order his execution … though not as much as it upset Essex.

Elizabeth's "wedding" ring

Elizabeth was the last Tudor because she never married and had children. Some people dared to hint that she should marry. Her reply was:

I have already joined myself in marriage to a husband, namely the kingdom of England.

77

Then she would show her coronation ring. She went on:
Do not blame me for the miserable lack of children; for everyone of you are children of mine.

But, when Elizabeth grew old and fat, the ring began to cut into her finger. She had to have it sawn off in January 1603. The superstitious Tudors saw this as a sign that her "marriage" to the country was ended. Two months later she was dead.

Not a lot of people know that ...

... Elizabeth was one of the cleanest women in England. She was proud of the fact that she took a bath once every three months. One person was amazed and reported that she had four baths a year *whether she needed it or not*! (Even 100 years later King Louis XIV of France only had three baths in his whole life!)

... Elizabeth was a fan of an early sort of five-a-side tennis ...
About three o'clock, ten men hung up lines in a square grass court in front of her majesty's windows.

They squared out the form of the court making a cross line in the middle. Then in this square (having taken off their doublets) they played five on each side, with a small ball, to the great liking of her highness ...

Queen Elizabeth owned the first wristwatch in the world. Perhaps she lost it, because her dying words were ...

All my possessions for a moment of time.

Terrible Tudor joke ...

The Tudors were Henry VII, Henry VIII, Edward VI and Mary ... but who came after Mary?

Answer:
Her little lamb.

Terrible Tudor witches

Black cats and broomsticks

Witches casting magic spells then flying off on their broomsticks. They make great stories. But few people believe them today. The Tudors, though, thought that witches were capable of anything. And unfortunately for the so-called witches, the Tudors believed the best way to deal with a witch was to burn him or her. (Seven out of every ten people accused of being witches were women.) Some "witches" believed they would be spared if they admitted they were witches. In 1565 Elizabeth Francis confessed…

I learnt this art of witchcraft at the age of twelve years from my grandmother. She told me to renounce God and his word and to give my blood to Satan. She gave me Satan in the form of a white spotted cat. She taught me to feed the cat with bread and milk and to call it by the name of Satan.

When I first had the cat Satan I asked it to make me rich. He promised me I should and asked what I would like (for the cat spoke to me in a strange, hollow voice). I said, "Sheep," and this cat at once brought 18 sheep to my pasture, black and white. They stayed with me for a time, but in the end did all vanish away. I know not how.

I then asked for a husband, this Francis whom I now have, and the cat promised that I should have him. We were married and had a child but we did not live as quietly as I'd hoped. So I willed Satan to kill my six-month old child and he did.

When I still could not find a quiet life I asked it to make my husband lame. It did it in this way. It came one morning to Francis' shoe, lying in it like a toad. As he put on the shoe he touched it with his foot and he was taken with a lameness that will not heal.

Elizabeth said that she gave the cat to her friend Agnes Waterhouse. Agnes claimed that the cat ...

killed a pig
killed three of a priest's pigs
drowned a cow
drowned geese
killed a neighbour
killed her husband.

Elizabeth Francis went to prison for a year – by confessing to her witchcraft she saved her life. Agnes Waterhouse was hanged.

The truth about Margaret

If you were Margaret Harkett's judge you might decide …

1 William Goodwin hated the old woman because she was a beggar and a nuisance.

2 Goodwin's lamb must have been sick because healthy lambs aren't brought into the kitchen.

3 The lamb dying at the same time as Margaret's visit was just bad luck – coincidence.

You might also decide …

1 Mrs Frynde was upset and bitter at the death of her husband and wanted to blame someone.

2 Frynde's fall from the pear tree was bad luck.

3 It was odd that Frynde never mentioned the curse until he was dying.

4 Frynde died of one of the many illnesses of those times or as a result of the fall.

Do you judge Margaret Harkett "Guilty" or "Not Guilty"? What did her judge do in 1585?

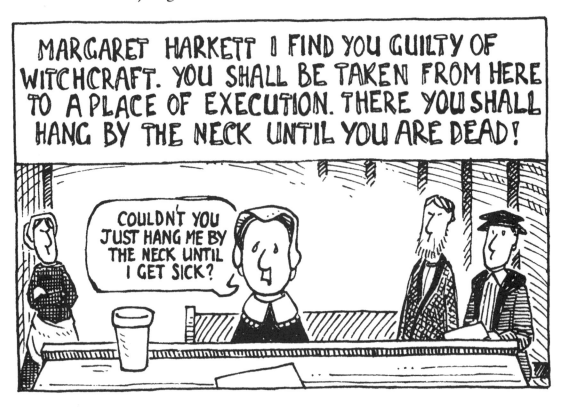

Margaret was executed. So were hundreds of other old women who were simply blamed for any accidents or illnesses in the area. They were usually alone – they had no one to stand up for them. They were usually too weak to stand up to their bullying neighbours.

Which is witch?

The Tudors had a way of testing a person for witchcraft. They would put the suspected witch into a sack and throw them into a nearby pond or stream. If s/he floated then s/he was a witch and would be taken out and executed. If s/he sank then s/he was innocent ... but probably dead from drowning.

Another test was to have the accused witch recite the *Lord's Prayer* without one mistake – could you do that, knowing that the first slip and you would die?

Witch fact...

In the sixteenth and seventeenth centuries about 100,000 people in Europe were accused of being witches and were killed.

Witchcraft laws

Witchcraft wasn't seen as particularly serious until 1542, when it became punishable by death if it was used for …

… discovering treasure

… injuring others

… unlawful love

In 1569 a list of magical practices that were banned included …

… curing men or beasts

… summoning wicked spirits

… telling where things were lost

Tudor superstitions

The death rate from disease was very high in Tudor times. Babies were especially likely to die from an illness. With so much death around the Tudors tried their own type of "witchcraft" to keep death and bad luck away. They didn't call their actions "witchcraft" - they called it "superstition". Some of the things they believed may seem odd to us today. They believed …

… when a baby was born they must ring church bells to frighten away evil spirits. Sometimes evil fairies stole the child and left a wicked fairy child in its place (a changeling).

... it was unlucky to wrap a new-born baby in new clothes, so it spent the first few hours of its life wrapped in an old cloth or in the clothes of older brothers or sisters. The baby had to be carried upstairs before it was carried downstairs.

... the twelfth night after Christmas was another time when evil spirits were flying around - protect yourself by chalking a cross on the beams of your house.

... it was unlucky if a hare ran in front of you - **hares**, they thought, were one of the shapes that a witch took to get around the country quickly! (Witches also disguised themselves as cats, dogs, rats, toads, wasps or butterflies. They would be fed with milk, bread and blood sucked from the witch.)

... it was unlucky to leave empty eggshells lying about - they could become a witch's boat.

... in an ancient way to tell your fortune. You had to jump over a lighted candle. If the candle stayed lit then good luck was coming . . . but if the candle went out then bad luck was sure to follow. Which nursery rhyme describes this fortune-telling method?

Answer:
Jack be nimble, Jack be quick,
Jack jump over the candlestick

Witch ghosts

In Buxted, Sussex, there is a lane called Nan Tuck's Lane. Nan Tuck had been accused of being a witch and the villagers tried to drown her. Nan escaped but was later found hanging in a nearby wood. Her ghost can be still seen running to the safety of the church, along Nan Tuck's Lane.

It is said that the screams of witches tortured by the witch-finder general can be heard in the dead of night at Seafield Bay in Suffolk.

Anne Chattox, the head of a group of Lancashire witches, was accused of digging up three skulls from a churchyard to use in a spell. She was hanged.

Father Ambrose Barlow's skull can be seen not far away, at Wardley Hall in Lancashire. He was a Catholic priest who died for his faith. The legend goes that this skull must not be disturbed in any way ... or else it will give the most blood-chilling scream you ever heard!

Terrible Tudor food

Foul facts on food

Tudor women, men and children in England drank beer, wine, sherry (or "sack"), mead and cider. This was not because they were drunkards. It was because the water was not fit to drink unless boiled.

The rich could buy or hunt for a wide range of meats. The poor had very little meat. Their main food was bread. Sometimes they caught rabbits, hares or fish to go with their turnips, beans and cabbage.

Tudor people were keen on spices. Most of the food was heavily salted to stop it going bad, so spices helped to disguise the salty taste. It also disguised the taste of rotten meat! Cinnamon, cloves, garlic and vinegar were all used.

Sugar was a rare luxury but, when they could get some, they used it on most of their food … including meat! Their other means of sweetening food was with honey.

Hot cross buns were made at Easter- but not always eaten – they were kept as luck charms instead!

Sailors had too much salt meat and not enough fresh vegetables on their long sea journeys. As a result they developed a disease called scurvy. Their gums began to rot, their breath to smell and their teeth began to drop out. Henry VIII's ship, the *Mary Rose*, was sunk in 1545 but recovered in 1982. The sailors had drowned, but modern-day tests show that many were already dying of scurvy.

People who went to see a play would usually eat while they watched. The actors could be really put off by people cracking nuts or trampling on the shells while they tried to act!

Four-and-twenty blackbirds baked in a pie? Not so daft a rhyme. Tudors and Stuarts loved eating birds - favourites were peacocks, larks and seagulls. And not just dead birds. This incredible recipe was included in a cookery book…

TO MAKE PIES THAT THE BIRDS MAY BE ALIVE IN THEM AND FLY OUT WHEN IT IS CUT UP

Make the piecrust of a great pie.
Fill it full of flour and bake it.
Being baked, open a hole at the bottom and take out the flour.
Then having a real pie the size of the hole, put it inside the piecrust. Put under the piecrust, around the real pie, as many small live birds as the empty piecrust will hold.
This to be done before such a time as you send the pie to the table and set it before the guests
Uncovering, or cutting up the great lid of the pie, all the birds will fly out, which is a delight and a pleasure to the guests.
So that they may not be hungry, you shall cut open the small pie.   ye woman's weekly pg 76

Got that? A big, **fake** piecrust covers a small, **real** pie **and** a flock of birds, yes? But the recipe doesn't explain what the birds are doing to the small pie – or what they are doing on the small pie – while they are waiting to be released.

Tudor foods you may want to eat

EGGS IN MUSTARD SAUCE

Ingredients:
Eggs – one for each person
& for each egg –
25 g butter
5 ml mustard (1 teaspoon)
5 ml vinegar (1 teaspoon)
A pinch of salt

Cooking:
Boil the eggs for 5 to 6 minutes.
While the eggs are boiling put the butter in a small saucepan and heat it.
When the butter has melted and begins to turn brown, take it off the heat.
Stir in the salt, mustard and vinegar.
When the eggs are ready remove the shells, cut them into quarters and put them on a warm dish.
Heat up the sauce again and pour it over the eggs.

ye womans weekly pg 77

JUMBLES (KNOTTED BISCUITS)

Ingredients:

2 eggs   15 ml aniseed or caraway (3 teasp)
100 sugar   175g plain flour

Cooking :

Beat the eggs. Add the sugar and aniseed (or caraway) and beat again. Stir in the flour to make a thick dough. Knead the dough on a floured board. Make the dough into rolls 1cm wide by 10cm long. Tie the strips into a single knot. Drop the knotted dough (6 at a time) into a pan of boiling water. They will sink to the bottom so use a spoon after a minute to help them float to the top. When the knots have floated for a minute and swelled, take them out of the water and let them drain on a wire rack. Put the knots on buttered baking sheets and bake for 15 minutes at Gas Mark 4 (or 350 degrees F. or 180 degrees C.). Turn them over and bake for another 10 minutes until they are golden brown.

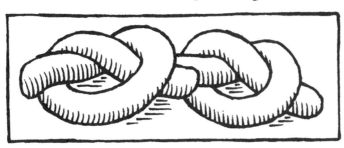

page 106

92

A Tudor guide to table manners

Do you ever get nagged for your behaviour at the dinner table? So did Tudor children. These complaints may sound familiar. A 1577 Tudor book suggested…

At the table you must…
not make faces
Scratch not thy head with thy fingers when thou art at meat.
not shout
Fill not thy mouth too full, lest thou perhaps must speak.
not gulp down drink too fast
Pick not thy teeth with thy knife nor with thy finger end.
not shuffle feet
not blow on food to cool it
Nor blow out thy crumbs when thou dost eat.
not take all the best food for yourself
Foul not the place with spitting where thou dost sit.

Terrible Tudor greed

The rich would eat much more than the poor. One feast for Henry VIII at Greenwich Palace lasted seven hours. Breakfast for the poor would be boringly the same every day – bread and ale; sometimes porridge made with peas or beans.

The tables of the rich would be laid with the usual salt, bread, napkins, spoons and cups. But each guest used his or her own knife.

And where were the plates? They used large slabs of bread called "trenchers" instead. The food was served straight onto that.

Every type of fish, meat and pastry was eaten, along with 20 types of jelly. The jellies were made into the shapes of castles and animals of various descriptions.

In November 1531, Henry had five banquets at which he and his guests ate…

24 beefs
100 fat muttons
51 great veals
34 porks
91 pigs
over 700 cocks and hens
444 pigeons
168 swans
over 4000 larks.

YOU SHOULD HAVE SEEN YESTERDAY'S BREAKFAST

Many dishes were more for show than eating. A peacock would be skinned, roasted, then put back into its skin for serving. A "cockatrice" would be made by sewing the front half of a cockerel onto the back half of a baby pig before roasting.

Terrible Tudor fun and games

Blood sports

In the Middle Ages people worked long hours, but they had as much as one day in three as a holy day (a saint's day usually) or holiday. What did they do?

And what did they do on those long dark winter nights? No television or radio or records or cinema. They played sports, played games and watched sports. Some are quite similar to today's. Others are very, very different!

Animal torture

In Southwark, London, there are two bear gardens with bears, bulls and other beasts to be baited in a plot of ground for the beholders to stand safe.

A 1599 report described this "sport" …
Every Sunday and Wednesday in London there are bear baitings. The bear pit is circular with stands around the top for spectators. The ground space down below is empty.
Here a large bear on a rope was tied to a stake. Then a number of great English Mastiff dogs were brought in and shown to the bear.
After this they baited the bear, one after the other. Although the dogs were struck and mauled by the bear they did not give in. They had to be pulled off by sheer force and their mouths forced open with long sticks. The bear's teeth were not sharp and they could not injure the dogs; they have them broken short.

When the first mastiffs tired, fresh ones were brought in to bait the bear. When the bear was tired a powerful white bull was then brought in. One dog at a time was set on him. He speared these with his horns and tossed them so they could not get the better of him. And, as the dogs fell to the floor again, several men held sticks under them to break their fall. Lastly they brought in an old, blind bear which boys hit with canes and sticks. But he knew how to untie his lead, and he ran back to his stall.

The audience might bet on which one would win.

In Congleton, Cheshire, the town had its own bear. The bear died in 1601. There is a story that the Corporation wanted a new one but didn't have the money . . . so they ordered the town bible to be sold to pay for it!

Football

Rules:

The pitch – could be the land between one village and the next – even if it is several miles. The ball – a pig's bladder or a ball of rags. Scoring – the team that gets the ball back to their village is the winner. Referee – none. Playing rules – none. Get the ball any way you can.

Match Commentary …

Doesn't every player in a football game lie in wait for his opponent, seeking to knock him down or punch him on the nose? Sometimes the players' necks are broken, sometimes their backs, sometimes their arms and legs are thrust out of joint, and sometimes their noses gush with blood.

Hunting for fish

The rich used to hunt for small animals using trained hawks. But there was also a sport of using birds to hunt for fish. First a cormorant, a diving sea bird, was trained to come back to its owner. When it was trained its head was covered with a mask and it was taken to the sea. At the sea shore it was unmasked and allowed to fly over the sea with a leather band around its neck. When it caught a fish it would return to the owner... but the poor bird couldn't swallow the fish because the leather band was fastened too tight. The owner simply took the fish from the poor cormorant's beak!

Public executions

Very popular. The person to be executed would always dress in their finest clothes and make a speech so the spectators felt they had been to a good "show".

Play it yourself

Stoolball (Tudor Cricket)

1 Pitch two posts about four metres apart.
2 Use a bundle of rags for a ball.
3 Use a stick as a bat.

The bowler tries to stand at one post and hit the other post with the ball, while the batter tries to hit the ball. If the bowler hits the post then the batter is "out" and the next member of the team has a turn. If the batter hits the ball to a fielder he can be caught out.

The batter scores by hitting the ball and running from post to post and back again. The team that scores the most runs is the winner.

Loggats

Plant a stick in the ground, a "stake". Each player takes turns in throwing smaller sticks, "loggats". The player whose "loggat" finishes nearest the "stake" is the winner. You can invent your own scoring system.

Tame games

Table games

Dice, cards, dominoes, backgammon, chess and draughts were popular in Tudor times as they are today.

Here are some Tudor games you can try for yourself…

Hazard

You need two dice and any number of players.

1 Everyone throws two dice. The highest scorer is the "Caster".

2 The Caster throws until s/he gets 5, 6, 7, 8 or 9. The number s/he gets is the "Main Point".

3 The Caster throws again until s/he gets a number 4, 5, 6, 7, 8, 9 or 10. This is the "Chance Point". The "Chance Point" cannot be the same as the "Main Point".

4 The Caster throws again and tries to get the Chance Point – if s/he does then s/he is the winner.

5 If the Caster throws the "Main Point" before s/he manages to throw another "Chance Point" then s/he loses.

6 Use matchsticks to gamble with. If the Caster wins, s/he takes one matchstick from each player. If the Caster loses then s/he pays out a matchstick to each other player.

7 Once the Caster loses s/he passes the dice to the next player who throws for a new "Main Point" and a new "Chance Point".

Trump

You need a pack of playing cards and two or more players.

1 Place a pack of cards on the table face down.

2 Turn one card over. That number card is the "Trump".

3 Each person, one at a time, will turn the other cards over.

4 Every time one matches the "Trump", all the players hit the table with the left hand and shout "Trump!" Whoever is the last to shout and hit the table is out.

Merelles

You need a board marked like the one on page 101. Draw it onto a large piece of card.

You need ten counters, or coins, and two players.

1 Each player takes turns to place a counter on a dot.

2 The aim is to place three counters in a row.

3 If all the counters are on the board and there are no rows of three then the players can begin to move their counters.

4 A player can only move to an open dot and only one space each turn.

5 The first to get a row of three is the winner.

MERELLES BOARD

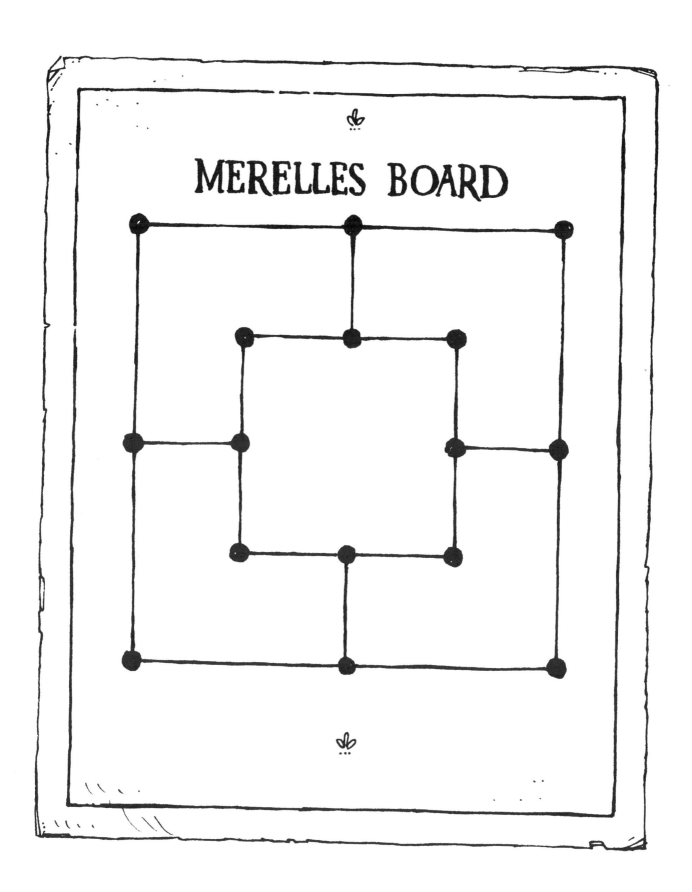

Some Tudor games you shouldn't play

Cudgelling

A game for two players.
1 Each is armed with a short stick.
2 The aim is to hit your opponent over the head.
3 A point is scored every time you make your opponent's head bleed!

NEXT TIME I GET THE BIG STICK!

Dun the cart-horse

A game for two equal teams.
1 The dun is a large log of wood, dragged to the centre of the village green and set upright.
2 The two teams start at opposite sides of the green. When one player shouts, "the dun is stuck in the mire," everyone rushes forward and tries to push the log over – while the other team is trying to push it over towards you.
The winning team is the one that succeeds.
But, beware! Anyone hit over the head with the log is said to be "Out" – not surprising, really!

Hurling

A game for two teams of 15 to 30 players.

1 A wooden ball is boiled in candle-grease to make it more slippery.

2 The aim is to pick up the ball and run through the other team's "goal".

3 If a player with the ball is tackled, he must pass the ball but he can only pass it backwards.

4 If your team don't have the ball then your aim is to stop the other team scoring – stop them any way you can!

Tudor sports reports

The Prior of Bicester Abbey has been paying money to players who play football on holidays. They are England's first professional footballers.

1491. Golf has been banned in Scotland by law because it's a wasteful pastime.
In no place in the country shall there be football, golf or other such unprofitable sports.

1513. King Henry VIII is so keen on bowling at Skittles that he took a portable bowling alley with him on a trip to France.

Terrible Tudor sailors

The sailors of Tudor Times are legendary for their daring exploits - trips around the earth in little leaking boats, fighting the mighty Spanish, French and Dutch navies, roaming the oceans with piratical plots.

Sir Francis Drake was the scourge of the oceans. He raided the coasts of the Caribbean and South America, sucking the wealth from these Spanish territories. As Drake filled Queen Elizabeth's coffers with plundered gold, she gave him more and more little jobs to do, such as helping to defeat the great Spanish Armada in 1588. It is of no surprise that many legends have been woven round Drake's cunning exploits. And wherever there are legends there are lies. Could you sort out the historical from the hysterical?

Hearing and believing

Drake's Drum

From 1577 till 1580 Sir Francis Drake sailed around the world in the service of Elizabeth I. At last, in the West Indies in 1596, he lay dying. He sent for his drum, an instrument that his men believed had magical powers. He ordered that it be sent back to England. He swore that he would return to defend his homeland if anyone beat the drum when England was in danger.

The drum was taken back to Buckland Abbey near Plymouth, where it remains to this day. The legend has changed a little over the years. The drum beats out its own warning when the country is in danger.

The drum is said to have rattled when Napoleon Bonaparte was brought to Plymouth after the battle of Waterloo. It seemed to know that the great enemy of England was nearby.

Then it has been heard three times this century. It sounded in 1914 when the first World War started; it sounded towards the end of that war when it had been taken on board the Royal Navy flagship, *The Royal Oak*.

When it sounded on *The Royal Oak*, the German fleet were approaching. They were heading towards the British fleet in order to surrender … perhaps it was giving a "Victory" salute.

Men were sent twice to find out where the noise of the drum was coming from – and twice they returned with no answer. The commander searched the ship for himself … and found nothing. Every sailor was at battle-stations in the ship. No one could have played the drum. *The Royal Oak* dropped anchor.

The drum-roll stopped as mysteriously as it had started.

The last time the drum was heard was in the darkest hours of World War Two. The British forces had crossed the channel to attack Hitler's German army. They were being driven back to the beaches. The German army was closing in, ready to massacre them. A miracle was needed.

The drum was heard sounding – the miracle occurred! A fleet of little British boats set off from the fishing ports and coastal towns of Eastern England. Somehow they crossed the channel, rescued huge numbers of men, then brought them safely home.

Was Sir Francis Drake watching over this feat of sea bravery, which was surely as great as his own trip round the world?

The Spanish Armada – Who won? Who lost?

The Spanish Armada, its special date
Is fifteen hundred and eighty-eight.

King Philip II of Spain was fed up with the English. His wife had been Mary I, Queen of England. He reckoned that he should be king, now that she was dead. But Elizabeth had grabbed the throne.

Also, English sailors were roaming the high seas and attacking the Spanish ships and colonies for their riches.

 Why was the Spanish Armada so expensive to run?

Because they only got 20 miles to the galleon.

Worse, Philip was Catholic and Elizabeth I was a Protestant, chopping off Catholic heads. In 1587 she had Mary Queen of Scots executed. This was the last straw as far as Philip was concerned.

So, in 1588 he decided it was time to teach the English a lesson once and for all. He assembled a huge fleet, an "Armada" of 130 galleons, and sent his armies off to invade England. They failed. This is what happened...

Of 130 galleons that left Spain in the summer of 1588, only about 50 returned in late September. As many as 19,000 Spaniards are thought to have died – it took them so long to sail back to Spain that many who didn't drown starved instead.

But the English sailors had their problems, too. In August 1588 the English Admiral, Lord Howard, wrote…

The sailors cry out for money and know not when they are to be paid. I have given them my word and honour that l will see them paid. If I had not done so they would have run away from Plymouth in their thousands.

But worse was to follow. Just the next day, Howard was writing…

Sickness and death begin to wonderfully grow among us. It is a most pitiful sight to see, here at Margate, how the men, having no place to go, die in the streets. It would grieve any man's heart to see them that have served so bravely to die so miserably.

So, Elizabeth won – she kept her throne. But who really lost? The English sailors? The Spanish sailors? Or both?

Sir Walter Raleigh

Sir Walter Raleigh was a sailor, too … **and** a writer, **and** explorer. He was a favourite of Queen Elizabeth I. A lot of stories have been told about him … but are they all true?

Try these questions on your teacher. All they have to answer is 'True" or "False".

1 Walter Raleigh once spread his cloak in the mud for Queen Elizabeth to walk over.
True or False?

2 Walter Raleigh was the first man to bring potatoes to England. *True or False?*

3 Walter Raleigh was the first man to bring tobacco to England. *True or False?*

Answer:
All are false!

110

The Truth About Walter

1 Most people have heard the story of Sir Walter Raleigh and the cloak. It was supposed to have happened when Raleigh was a young man. The queen was passing through crowds of her people when she reached a muddy puddle in the road. She stopped. After all, she didn't want to spoil her fine shoes.

Quick-thinking Walter Raleigh pulled off his new cloak and covered the puddle so she could step over without walking through mud. The queen smiled. Walter's act was to make him a rich and powerful favourite of the queen.

A great story. But a true story? No. It originated with Thomas Fuller who was a historian of the 17th century who liked to "dress up" boring history with lively little incidents like the story of Raleigh's cloak ... even if they didn't really happen!

2 Walter Raleigh's potatoes? For hundreds of years Walter Raleigh teachers have taught that Raleigh brought the first potatoes to England when he returned from a voyage to America in 1586. But there is no evidence from Tudor times to say this happened. A book called *Herball* (written by John Gerard in 1597) talks about someone called Clusius who had grown potatoes in Italy in 1585. The vegetable became very popular and was grown everywhere in Europe within ten years.

3 Walter Raleigh's tobacco? Again there are records of tobacco being used in France in 1560 – 26 years before Raleigh's ships returned from Virginia. It was brought there by John Nicot (whose name gives us "Nicotine"). It must have crossed the English Channel long before Raleigh's ships even set off.

In 1573 William Harrison wrote...

In these days the taking in of the Indian herb called "Tobacco" is greatly taken up in England. It is used against rheums and other diseases of the lungs with great effect.

But not everyone agreed. In 1614, Barnaby Rich was writing...

They say tobacco is good for a cold, rheums, for aches, for dropsies and for all manner of diseases. But I see the ones who smoke most are as affected by those diseases as much as the ones who don't. It is now sold in every tauern, inn and ale-house as much as beer.

Oddly enough, the man who hated tobacco smoking the most was King James I. He wrote that smoking was...

A custom loathsome to the eye, hateful to the nose, harmful to the brain and dangerous to the lungs.

(If Raleigh really **did** smoke and James I was the first anti-smoking campaigner, then James was a great success. In 1618 he cured Raleigh's "loathsome" habit for good. James had Raleigh's head cut off for treason!)

What is it?

Drake found some new foods on his journey round the world. But what were they?

1 *We found a plant with a fruit as big as a man's head. Having taken off the back (which is full of string) you shall come to a hard shell which holds a pint of sweet liquid. Within that shell you will find a white, hard substance as sweet as almonds and half an inch thick.*

2 *We found a store of great fowl which could not fly, the bigness of geese, whereof we killed 3000 in less than one day.*

Answers:
1 Coconuts, 2 Turkeys

Terrible Tudor clothes

Did you know?

It was during the Tudor period that English clothes for the rich became exciting and different. Merchants were in touch with countries as far away as Russia and America. While the Tudor poor still wore rough woollen clothes, the Tudor rich were better dressed than ever before with velvets and satins from Italy, lace from France and starch from Holland. And starch meant they could make those stiff collars, "Ruffs", that were so popular in Elizabeth's time. But…

Ten things you probably didn't know…

1 Sometimes the stiff ruffs were so wide that ladies couldn't reach their mouths to eat! Silversmiths had to make extra-long spoons for them.

2 Ruffs were usually white but could be another colour. Yellow ruffs were popular for a while. Then a famous murderess, Mrs Turner, was hanged wearing one. They suddenly went out of fashion!

3 A puritan, Philip Stubbes, claimed...

The devil invented these great ruffs. But if it happen that a shower of rain catch them, then their great ruffs fall, as dishcloths fluttering in the wind.

4 Henry VIII looks very fat in his portraits. But as well as having an over-fed body, his clothes were thick with padding- at least it kept him warm in his draughty castles.

5 The Elizabethan ladies' fashion was for tiny waists. To help them squeeze into smart dresses, the ladies (and even the girls) wore iron corsets.

6 Girls showed that they were unmarried by wearing no hat in public.

7 Elizabethan men wore short trousers called "hose". They had to pad them so they wouldn't show any creases. They weren't too fussy what they padded them with - horsehair (itchy!), rags or even bran (horsefood)! If the "hose" split the bran would run

8 Poor country girls often wore shoes with iron rings under them. Sometimes they had thick wooden soles. This was to keep their skirts out of the deep mud and rubbish in the streets and market places.

EARLY PLATFORMS

9 In 1571, Elizabeth's parliament made a law forcing all married women to wear white knitted caps, and all men (over the age of six) to wear woollen hats. The caps and hats had to be knitted in England using English wool. Elizabeth got a lot of taxes from the wool trade – English wool was in great demand from other countries, too.

10 Aprons were quite a new idea in Tudor times. You could often tell a man's occupation from the design of his apron...

millers and cooks	– white
barbers	– checked
builders and blacksmiths	– leather

Terrible Tudor trousers

If you'd like to act like a Tudor, feel like a Tudor, or if you're off to a fancy dress party, you may like to try making these Tudor "hose".

1 Wear a pair of tights or tight trousers first.

2 Take a pair of old, baggy trousers. Cut them off at the knee. Slit them as shown.

3 Put the baggy trousers on over the tights. Tie them at the knee with ribbon or a scarf.

4 Stuff the baggy trousers with material of a different colour so it shows through the slits.

5 Wear a loose shirt and ruff and a belt with a sword or dagger - wooden, of course.

6 Go around saying, *To be* or *not to be*, or *Alas, poor Yorick*. (They're famous lines from William Shakespeare plays - adults and teachers will be totally impressed.)

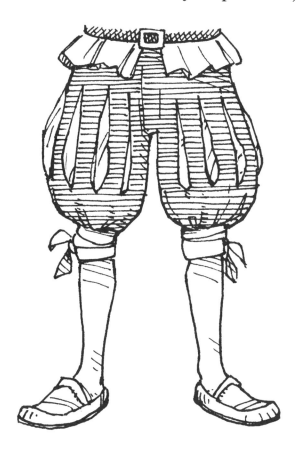

A ruff idea

1 Take seven 24 cm doilies (lacey paper table decorations, usually used at parties).

2 Cut them in half.

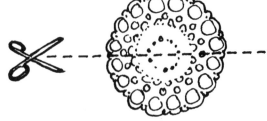

Use sticky tape to attach them to a 4 m strip of ribbon, allowing enough ribbon to tie at the back.

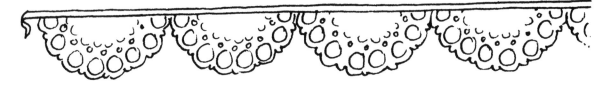

3 Make 2 cm folds in the doilies folding each one into a fan shape.

4 Keep the folds in place at the ribbon end with small stitches or sticky tape.

5 Tie the ends of the ribbon around your neck.

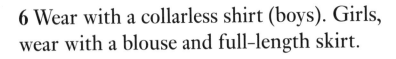

6 Wear with a collarless shirt (boys). Girls, wear with a blouse and full-length skirt.

7 Stroll around singing *Greensleeves*.

Terrible Tudor life for women

A woman's life is hard in ten terrible ways...

1 Girls could marry at 12 (boys at 14). This was usually arranged by their parents. They would still live with their parents at this age, though.

2 Many upper-class girls were married by 15. At the age of 16 they could live with their husbands.

3 It wasn't usually considered worth the money to send a girl to school. Her mother could teach her all the household crafts she would need to be a useful wife.

4 If a girl didn't marry there wasn't much she could do. The convents had been abolished by Henry VIII so she couldn't become a nun. Very often, unmarried girls would have to stay at home with their parents and spin. That's why they became known as "spinsters" – a word we still use.

JUST BECAUSE I DIDN'T GET MARRIED WHEN I WAS STILL PLAYING WITH MY TEDDY MEANS I'VE GOT TO SIT AND SPIN FOR THE REST OF MY LIFE

5 One farmer described a good wife's behaviour. He said she should…

pray when first getting out of bed, then clean the house, lay the table, milk the cows, dress her children, cook meals for the household, brew and bake when needed, send corn to the mill, make butter and cheese, look after the swine and collect the eggs.

6 Anthony Fitzherbert added to that list and said she should…
shear corn and in time of need help her husband to fill the dung cart, drive the plough, load hay and go to market to sell butter, cheese, milk, eggs, chickens, pigs, geese and all manner of corn.
(What did he expect her to do in her spare time?!)

7 But English women were better off than those in other countries – at least, that's what the men said! Thomas Platter said that…
the womenfolk of England have more freedom than in any other land. The men must put up with such ways and may not punish them for it. Indeed, the good wives often beat the men.

8 Girls were expected to help in the house by collecting fine feathers (down) for mattresses, making candles, spinning, weaving and embroidering. Once every three months, the household tablecloths and bed-clothes were washed; the girls were expected to help with this.

9 Women could be punished for nagging or "scolding". A court record from 1592 says...

The wife of Walter Hycocks and the wife of Peter Phillips are common scolds. Therefore it is ordered that they shall be told in church to stop their scolding. But, if their neighbours complain a second time, they shall be punished by the ducking stool.

And "the ducking stool" meant being tied to a chair and lowered into a nearby river.

10 If the ducking stool didn't work then there was the "branks" – an iron mask that clamped onto the head with a metal bar going into the woman's mouth to hold her tongue down. Wearing the branks, a woman would be paraded round the town to show other women what might happen to them.

Miss World – Tudor style

The Elizabethans had a clear idea of what a beautiful woman should look like. Here's a shopping list...

1 extremely white skin
2 blue eyes
3 ruby-red lips
4 fair hair

You don't fit the description? Never mind, you can always change if you want.

Dark hair can be bleached with a mixture of sulphur and lead. This will, unfortunately, make it fall out in time. Never mind, as an Elizabethan said, Elizabethan girls are ...
not simply content with their own hair, but buy other hair either of horse, mare or any other strange beast,

Skin too dark? A deadly mixture of lead and vinegar can be plastered on. (This has the same effect as making an Egyptian mummy.)

Lips too pale? Lipstick could be made from egg whites and cochineal - what is "cochineal"? It's a dye made from crushed cochineal beetles.

THREE SIMPLE STEPS TO A MORE BEAUTIFUL YOU!

Eyes don't sparkle enough? Drop in some belladonna (which means, "beautiful lady"!) to make them look larger. Keep it away from your lips, though. Belladonna is a poisonous drug made from deadly-nightshade.

If a mother wanted her daughter to grow up beautiful she was advised to bathe her in milk to give her a pale skin. Unwanted freckles? (Definitely out of fashion.) Treat with "brimstone" (sulphur).

Smelly? **Don't** have a bath! (Baths aren't considered "healthy"!) Just cover up the smell with perfume.

So…

Would you like to have been a Tudor woman or girl? In fact, would you have liked to live in the Terrible Tudor times at all? The Golden Age" of Good Queen Bess and Jolly Old Henry VIII?

Every age has its problems. But, as a historian once said…
In reviewing the past I think that we of the present day have much to be thankful for.

You've reviewed some of the Tudor past in this book. So, are you "thankful" that you didn't live then? Or do you agree with the history book that said it was an extremely exciting time to be alive?

Epilogue

Old Elizabeth died and the last of the terrible Tudors was gone. Mary Queen of Scots was dead too ... but her son, James VI of Scotland, was very much alive. The first of the sinister Stuarts.

The Stuart family in Scotland had a history every bit as bloody and violent as the Tudors in England.

• James I was murdered in a toilet in 1437 while he was trying to defend himself with a pair of fire tongs

• James II was killed by an exploding cannon in the seige of Roxburgh in 1460

• James III was murdered by his nobles in 1486

• James IV was killed at the Battle of Flodden in 1513

• James V died of despair shortly after his defeat at the battle of Solway Floss in 1542.

• Mary Queen of Scots, as we already know, murdered her husband then fled to England to avoid the chop. Elizabeth gave it to her instead

• James VI became the first James of England ... and the first lucky Stuart to come from Scotland. He came south and added the English throne to his collection.

Of course, not everyone was happy with James. Not everyone wanted a king with such disgusting habits! For a start, he picked his nose!

James always wore a dagger-proof vest. Who can blame him? First, some cunning Catholics tried to blow him off the throne with the gunpowder plot. Lucky James survived again! We may forget James, but we always remember the fifth of November!

And that was just the start of a dramatic century. A century of plagues and fire and plots and rebels; a century with Englishmen fighting Englishmen and Englishmen hanging witches - the Scots preferred to burn them!

If the Tudors gave their queens a sharp pain in the neck then the Stuart people gave it to one of their kings!

The Stuart times were certainly sinister. But that's another story, and another slice of Horrible History...

TERRIBLE TUDORS

GRISLY QUIZ

Now find out if you're a
terrible Tudor expert!

HORRIBLE HENRY

Henry VIII was one of Britain's cruellest monarchs ever. Here's a quick quiz to test your brains. Get one wrong and your head goes on the block…

THAT'S WHAT YOU GET WHEN YOU TAKE ON A TUDOR!

1. When wife no. 1, Catherine of Aragon, died Henry had a…?
a) ball
b) fight
c) cup of tea

2. Wife no. 2, Anne Boleyn, needed the toilet a lot during her coronation. Her ladies-in-waiting kept her potty handy…?
a) under the table
b) in a room close by
c) on the throne

3. When Anne gave birth to a daughter, Henry…?
a) sulked
b) cheered
c) fell out of his pram

4. While Anne was being beheaded, Henry was playing…?
a) tennis
b) music
c) the fool

5. Henry divorced wife no. 4, Anne of Cleves, because she was…?
a) ugly
b) stupid
c) vegetarian

6. Wife no. 5, Catherine Howard, was sentenced to death for having lovers. She begged for mercy but Heartless Henry locked the door and left her...?
a) to wail
b) in jail
c) looking pale

7. Henry had his old friend Thomas More executed and his head stuck...?
a) over London Bridge
b) under London Bridge
c) in a fridge

8. Henry had Cardinal Fisher beheaded and showed disrespect by leaving the headless body...?
a) naked for a day
b) on the main highway
c) in a window display

INGENIOUS INSULTS

Can you match the words in these columns to come up with ten insults that Shakespeare put into his plays? WARNING: Do NOT call your teacher any of these names.

1. taffeta	**a)** lump
2. scurvy	**b)** ape
3. red–tailed	**c)** chuff
4. threadbare	**d)** bumble-bee
5. mad–headed	**e)** punk
6. fat	**f)** juggler
7. false	**g)** crookback
8. bloodsucker of	**h)** caterpillars
9. scolding	**i)** sleeping men
10. deformed	**j)** lord

QUICK QUESTIONS - MEAN QUEENS

1. Catholic Mary came to the throne in 1553, and the Protestants showed what they thought of her by leaving something on her bed. What? (Clue: hounding her out of the palace?)

2. Mary married Spanish Prince Philip in 1554. He hated something that came from her nose. What? (Clue: 'snot what you think)

3. Philip left Mary and went to fight in Europe. She tried to tempt him back with what? (Clue: the way to a man's heart is through his stomach, they say)

4. Mary had a lot of Protestant 'heretics' burned. Her chief helper was Reginald Pole who chose really odd 'heretics' to burn. What was odd about them? (Clue: they never felt a thing)

5. Mary sent Archbishop Cranmer to the stake in 1556. He had written an apology then changed his mind. When he saw the fire he did a strange thing. What? (Clue: he went to his death single-handed)

6. Mary died and the news was taken to half-sister Elizabeth, the new queen. They say Elizabeth was reading in the garden when the news came, but that's unlikely. Why? (Clue: remember, remember when Mary died)

7. Elizabeth had a new tax created which only men could pay. It was a tax on what? (Clue: it might grow on you)

8. Elizabeth I's godson, Sir John Harrington, disgraced himself by making rude remarks to her ladies-in-waiting. She banished him. He

went off and invented something that was so useful she forgave him. What? (Clue: flushed with success?)

9. In 1576 the explorer Martin Frobisher returned to England with a load of 'black earth'. What use did he think it would be? (Clue: he thinks the soil is rich)

10. Eloye Mestrell invented the first machine in England for making coins for the government. Yet in 1578 he was arrested and executed. What was his crime? (Clue: double your money)

11. Mary Queen of Scots had Sir John Huntly beheaded but then discovered he had to be tried properly and found guilty if she was to get his fortune. What did she do? (Clue: head on over to the courtroom)

12. Mary Queen of Scots became unpopular in Scotland, and fled to England to ask cousin Elizabeth I for protection. How did Liz protect Mary? (Clue: no one can get in to get her)

13. James Douglas of Scotland invented the 'Maiden' machine. In 1581 the Maiden killed him. What was it? (Clue: a chip off the old block)

14. Mary Queen of Scots had lots of troubles. She finally met a man and thanked him for, 'making an end to all my troubles'. What was this man's job? (Clue: not an agony aunt!)

15. When Mary Queen of Scots was beheaded in 1587 her head was supposed to have been lifted high in the air by the executioner to prove she was dead. But he dropped it. Why? (Clue: hair today, gone tomorrow)

Would you believe it?

Queen Elizabeth I ruled from 1558 to 1603. There are lots of stories about this famous queen, but which of these tall tales are true and which false…?

1. She threatened to pass a law banning her courtiers from wearing long cloaks.
2. She died because of a rotten tooth.
3. Elizabeth was overjoyed when her sister, Mary, died.
4. She liked to read her horoscope.
5. Elizabeth ate a chessboard.
6. She had regular baths.
7. Elizabeth never even considered getting married.
8. Elizabeth had beautiful red hair.
9. She was always true to her Protestant faith.
10. She punched and kicked her secretary.

Answers

Horrible Henry
1–8. All answers are (a). Anyone answering (c) should give up quizzes ... now.

Ingenious insults
1.e) 2.j) 3.d) 4.f) 5.b) 6.c) 7.h) 8.i) 9.g) 10.a)

Quick Questions – Mean Queens
1. A dead dog. The head was shaved, the ears cropped and a noose put around its neck. The message was clear: 'This is what we do to Catholics.'

2. Philip hated Mary's foul breath. It was an illness she had and not her fault. But it put him off, and he left her broken hearted.

3. His favourite meat pies. She had them sent across the English Channel to him. He ate all the pies but didn't go home for more.

4. They were dead. Reggie dug them up and burned them anyway. Funny feller.

5. He stuck his writing hand in the flames to punish it for writing the apology. (No jokes about second-hand shops, please.)

6. It was November. Not many people are daft enough to sit in the garden in an English winter.

7. Beards.

8. A flushing toilet. It took him six years to invent it but Liz loved his loo.

9. He believed it contained a fortune in gold. It didn't. He was just a clueless captain.

10. Eloye made a second, secret, machine and forged money for himself. Usually forgers had a hand chopped off but Eloye was hanged.

11. Huntly's head was sewn back on and his corpse was put on trial.

12. Elizabeth locked Mary in prison. She left her there for years before deciding to execute her.

13. The Maiden was a type of guillotine. He was executed on it.

14. He was her executioner. Actually he made a messy end to her troubles, taking three chops and a bit of sawing to get the head off

15. Mary was wearing a wig. When he grabbed it, the head slipped out and bounced on to the floor.

Would you believe it?

1. True. She was terrified of being killed and wanted her courtiers' swords uncovered and ready.

2. False. Elizabeth is famous for having rotten teeth, but that didn't kill her. She caught a cold and never recovered.

3. True. She said, 'This is the Lord's doing and it is marvellous in our eyes.'

4. True. A mathematician (and magician!) called John Dee used to read Liz's horoscope and foretell the future for her.

5. True. Of course, it was made of marzipan.

6. True. Elizabeth did bathe regularly … once every three months!

7. False. Liz had a few close calls when it came to marriage, including Lord Dudley and the French Duke of Anjou.

8. True and False. She did at first, but she ended up bald with a collection of 80 wigs!

9. False. While Catholic Mary Tudor was queen, Elizabeth said she was a Catholic too.

10. True. Secretary William Davison was just one of the unfortunate palace workers who suffered Liz's temper tantrums.

INTERESTING INDEX

Where will you find 'blood-sucking fleas', 'smelly breath', 'swearing' and 'sewers' in an index? In a Horrible Histories book, of course!

This book is dedicated to all the readers around the world who have made Horrible Histories such a success. TD.

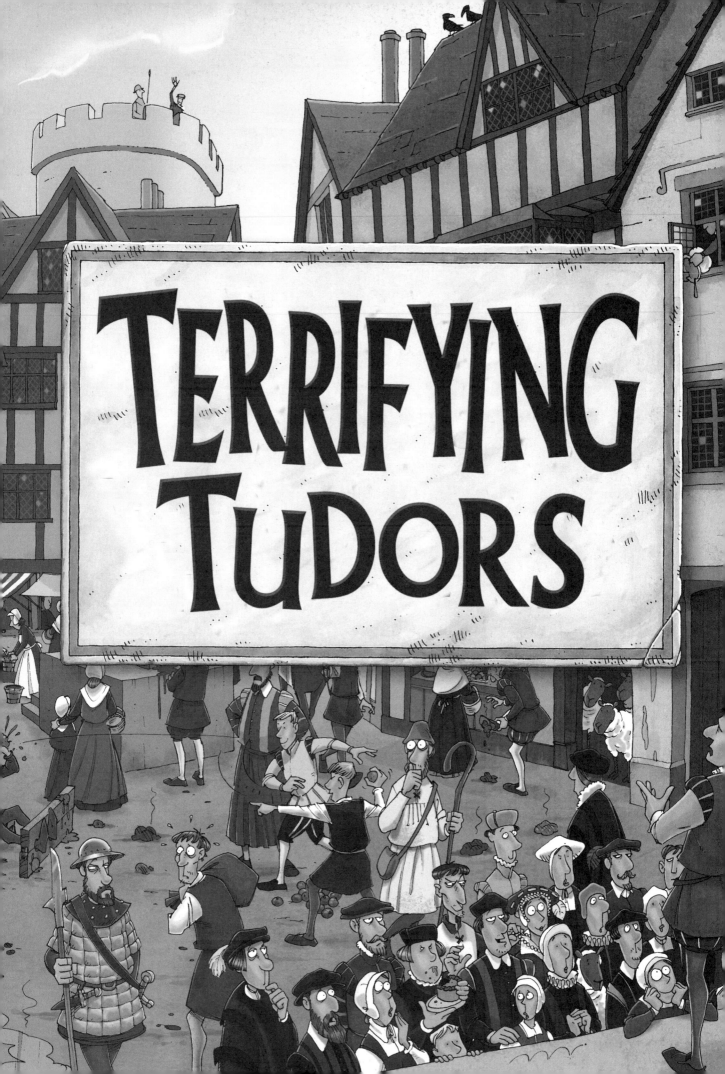

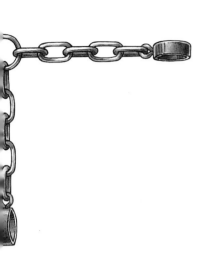

CONTENTS

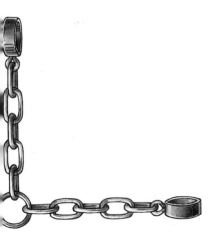

Introduction

History can be *horrible*. And who made it horrible? The vicious and cruel people who lived in the past.

And here's an amazing thing ... some of the most horrible people in history all had names beginning with the letter 'T'. Just look in your little sister's copy of *Tiddly Tots' Alphabet of Terrors*.

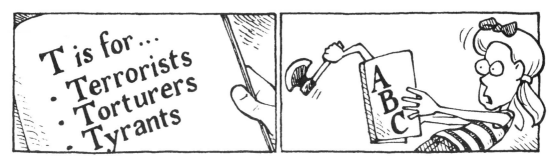

Or ask your teacher...

And the Tudors were truly terrifying torturing tyrants. Even worse than teachers!

The first Tudor had the bloodstained body of his defeated enemy tied to a horse and shown to the people. The message was clear...

The last Tudor had her boyfriend beheaded on a bloody block.

And, in between, there were thousands of people hanged, burned, boiled and chopped just to keep the Tudors on top.

In *The Terrible Tudors* there were foul facts about the fun loving Tudor family and their subjects. Now here are more savage stories of their suffering. Terrifying Tudors in fact. It would bring tears to the eyes of Tyrannosaurus rex. It may scare you witless, so be warned ... do *not* read this book with the lights out!

Henry the Mean Monarch

1485 Richard III is hacked to death at the Battle of Bosworth Field. His opponent, Henry Tudor, is crowned Henry VII. This man is ruthless ... and quite toothless too ... but not uthless when it comes to money. He makes England rich.

1509 Henry VII dies. All that money didn't do him much good. Never mind, his son, Henry VIII, will spend it for him on wine, women and wars.

King Henry VII (reigned 1485–1509)

In 1485 England was ruled by the last of the Plantagenet kings, Richard III. Richard was a hard-hearted man – he probably had his brother's children suffocated in the Tower of London.

> WEAK KINGS ONLY CAUSE TROUBLE AS STRONG LORDS SQUABBLE TO CONTROL THE COUNTRY. IMAGINE WHAT WOULD HAPPEN IF YOU HAD A 12-YEAR-OLD TEACHER FOR YOUR CLASS? CHAOS!

Ruthless Richard had his enemies – most kings did in those days. Those enemies looked around for someone to take Richard III's place.

There were 12 people in line to the throne but none could hope to beat Richard in battle. So Richard's enemies turned to the 13th in line to the throne – an almost unknown Welshman called Henry Tudor.

Henry landed in Wales with a small force and marched east. Richard gathered his army and marched west. They met in the middle and fought the Battle of Bosworth Field in Leicestershire. Richard's friends deserted him and went over to Henry Tudor's side.

Suddenly England had a Tudor king, Henry VII, and no one was as surprised as Henry. Then the battle began to hold on to his throne.

There were plenty of 'pretenders' who said they should be king, but only one got really close to stopping the Tudors in their tracks. A boy who may have been called Lambert Simnel. Sadly he never told his fantastic story. If he had it may have looked like this…

The king in the kitchen

Look at me in my rags and patches. A kitchen boy in King Henry's castle. I'm the boy that could have been king … I was *that* close! But don't feel sorry for me, sweating down here over the roast sheep and stuffed swans. I'm not complaining. I could be dead. In fact, I'm surprised I'm not!

I don't know who my parents were but I do know my teacher was a priest called William Simonds, and Father William hated Henry Tudor. 'The good people of England will rise against him!' he used to cry when he'd had a few flagons of wine.

'But who will be king then?' I asked. I was only ten years old and didn't understand.

'Edward, Earl of Warwick. Poor dead Richard III's nephew, of course,' the priest said.

I'd heard about Edward of Warwick. 'He's locked in the Tower of London,' I said. 'And he couldn't be king anyway. They say he's simple-minded.'

That's when Father William gripped my tunic and breathed wine in my face. 'But *you're* not simple-minded, my boy.

'You're the brightest pupil I've ever had.

You could *pretend* to be Edward of Warwick! You're the right age and you look a little like him. The rebel lords of England would follow you and smash that Welsh milksop Henry Tudor. You would be king!'

I was too young and frightened to argue. For a year he taught me all I needed to know about being Edward of Warwick. He told me how Edward's father, George of Clarence, had been drowned in a barrel of wine by 'my' dead Uncle Richard. After a year I almost began to believe it myself!

Then we went to Ireland to raise an army. Some of the rebel lords, like John, Earl of Lincoln, knew I was not Edward of Warwick. But the Irish believed the story. There were tears in their eyes when I told them of my escape from the Tower. Yet it was all lies. It's the Irish I felt most sorry for. My wild friends. I led them to their deaths, you know.

John of Lincoln had me crowned King Edward VI in Dublin, then we crossed into England and marched to meet Henry Tudor's army. We landed in the north of England because that's where Richard III's supporters were. But we didn't get the people following us the way we'd hoped. Just a few adventurous young men who were tired of herding sheep. They weren't trained soldiers.

We did have German soldiers who were paid to fight. With their crossbows and their pikes they were experts. They tried to train the shepherd lads. But they would never train the wild Irishmen. 'They fight with their long daggers and javelins,' John of Lincoln told me as we rode south. 'They have wooden shields and no armour. They just charge wildly at the enemy the way they did a thousand years ago when the Romans landed.'

'Won't they get hurt?' I asked.

He looked at me strangely. 'There would be no glory if there was no risk,' he said. 'They will be happy to die for you.'

'For me? But I'm only…'

'The rightful King of England,' he said sharply. 'And never forget it.'

On the morning of 16 June we stood on a hilltop near the village of Stoke. I looked across at Henry Tudor's army. Even I could see that behind their bright banners there were twice as many men as we had. I could make out Henry Tudor, riding in front of his troops and encouraging them.

My boy's voice was too weak, but I rode in front of the men and they cheered me. 'King Edward! King Edward!' they cried. Then

Lincoln took me away to watch from a safe spot at the top of a windmill. I watched my brave friends march forward, still chanting, 'King Edward!'

I wish I hadn't watched the battle. It wasn't glorious, the way John of Lincoln said. It was bloody and cruel. My Germans fired their crossbow bolts and stopped the front row of Henry Tudor's army. But Henry's archers fired back with their longbows till the sky was black with arrows. When they stopped, my Irish friends were dead or dying, spiked like hedgehogs with the steel-tipped arrows.

The Germans marched forward and died with their blood-soaked standards wrapped around them. My soldiers couldn't have run away if they tried.

They were cut off by fast horsemen and massacred in a narrow pass they call the Red Gutter – red with the blood of my friends. After three hours, when all was lost, I saw John of Lincoln ride boldly forward, only to be cut down by Henry Tudor's knights.

When a Tudor squire called Robert Bellingham came for me I was ready to die. I didn't want to live with the nightmare of what I'd just seen. But Henry Tudor was cruel. He had me brought before him. He was a thin, pale-faced man with bad teeth and small, cold eyes. He said, 'Who are you, boy?'

'Lambert Simnel,' I told him.

'Do you know what I'm going to do with you, little Lambert?'

'Execute me, sir,' I said.

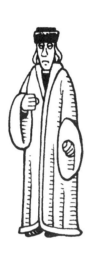 He leaned forward and smiled. 'No, boy. People would say I executed you because you were Edward of Warwick. As long as you're alive you can tell people the truth. You are just a foolish boy called Lambert Simnel.'

'Will you lock me in the Tower with the real Earl of Warwick?' I asked.

'It costs money to keep a prisoner. I have to pay for food and guards. No, you can stay here in Sheen Palace. In return for your life you can work for me here. A simple, but hard, life in the kitchens would suit you, I think.'

Part of me was glad to be alive. But at night, when the nightmares come and I hear the dying screams of the Battle of Stoke, then I wish I were dead.

Cruel Henry had the real Earl of Warwick put to death. But cruellest of all, he sentenced me to live.

Lambert Simnel became a faithful servant to Henry VII and, in time, was promoted to become the falconer to Henry VII's son, King Henry VIII. He was still alive 40 years after the Battle of Stoke.

Neither Henry VII nor any other English king rode out to face rebels on a battlefield again. A second pretender, Perkin Warbeck, tried to invade from Scotland but failed. Again Henry Tudor treated him with mercy. But foolish Warbeck kept plotting and Henry had to act. Warbeck was executed, along with the real Earl of Warwick, in 1499.

Did you know…?

Henry Tudor was always considered to be a 'lucky' king and he used this luck to argue, 'God is on my side.'

After the Battle of Stoke, for example, news got back to London that Henry had been defeated. A supporter of Lambert Simnel, John Swit, stood up and made a speech, claiming that Henry Tudor had got the death he deserved. Then, before he finished speaking, John Swit's face seemed to turn purple and then black and he dropped down dead! Henry Tudor was amused.

The crafty king

Henry Tudor was 'careful' with his money. The gossips in the palace said the Queen wore buckles of tin because the King was too mean to buy her silver. Her gowns were mended time and time again, frayed cuffs turned up and worn threads patched. They also said she had to borrow money from her servants.

But Henry was just as careful with his country's money as he was with his own. When the pretender, Perkin Warbeck, led an army to attack the country, Henry Tudor had to raise an army too. That cost money. The soldiers had to have weapons and food and they had to be fed.

Warbeck's army was defeated and Henry captured the rebel lords. He could have had them executed. Instead he fined them and let them go home to raise the money.

The bills for Henry's army came to £13,200. The lords paid him £14,700 in fines. So, Henry VII managed to make a £1,500 profit out of being attacked. That's crafty.

Horrible Henry

1509 Henry VIII takes the throne because his older brother, Arthur, has carelessly died. Big Hen not only takes Arthur's crown but his wife, Catherine, too. Henry loves sport, fighting, music and eating. Most of all he loves himself.

1536 Henry decides he wants rid of his old wife Cathy … so he puts himself in charge of the Church and grants himself a divorce. The old Catholic Church and its monks and monasteries are banned. Big Hen pockets their wealth, of course. And, of course, rebels get the chop. Soon he starts chopping wives, too (Anne Boleyn and Catherine Howard) and divorcing wives (Catherine of Aragon and Anne of Cleves). Favourite wife, Jane, dies giving birth to their son, Edward … who'll become the next Tudor king.

1547 Mad, bad Henry VIII dies (which saves a lot on the palace food bills). He leaves England poorer and divided, and sickly, nine-year-old Edward VI, in charge. Sad.

King Henry VIII (reigned 1509–1547)

Henry wasn't ruler of England because he was wise, strong and just. He was king because his father, Henry VII, had been king and his older brother, Arthur, had died.

Of course, if anyone had said in Tudor times that Henry was mad they'd have been playing football with their own head.

Henry reigned for 38 torturing Tudor years and, in that time, about 72,000 people were executed. That's about 1,900 a year, or five every day. It must have been a bit like a National Lottery with 35 losers every week.

Which of these topped Tudor victims would you like to have been?

Lottery of life losers

Margaret Pole, Countess of Salisbury – 1541
What would *you* do if an executioner said…

Would you do as you were told? Would you say, as you were supposed to, 'I forgive you, executioner,' and give him a bag of gold? Or would you be really rotten to the poor axeman, like the eccentric old Countess of Salisbury?

Henry VIII planned to visit York. He wanted the Tower of London empty of prisoners so none would escape while his back was turned. One of those prisoners was the Countess of Salisbury. When it was her turn to be executed, Henry's chief executioner, Master Cratwell, was away from London. The job was left to a boy. You have to feel sorry for him!

If the young executioner had written a letter home then it might have looked something like this...

Tower Green
London
1541

Dear Mum,
Started my new job as executioner today. It's not as easy as it looks! I have a nice uniform. Here's a picture I drew looking in a mirror:

You'd be proud of me — except you wouldn't know it was me 'cos Henry's executioners are ~~anommynus~~ ~~annunnymous~~ secret.
Anyway, the boss, Robert Cratwell (whose name I

can't tell you 'cos it's secret), said I could start with an easy one. 'It's the old Countess of Salisbury,' he said. 'She's nearly 70 years old so she'll be no trouble.'

'Seventy!' I said. 'If she gets any older her head'll probably just drop off!' I laughed. I didn't know the joke would be on me! 'What's the old trout done?' I asked.

'Nothing,' Robert said. 'She's never had a trial or been found guilty. But her son, Cardinal Pole, was a Catholic and he started stirring up trouble for the King. So Henry had the Cardinal's old mother thrown in the Tower a couple of years ago. And the King made sure she suffered in there with terrible food and no heating. The old woman will be glad to be out of it.'

Then he gave me a few last-minute lessons in chopping and sent me off to do some target-practice on a turnip. I was spot on. That turnip was sliced as neat as one that you'd put in your stew, Mum. But there was no one watching, was there? And turnips don't move.

Imagine the shock when I found dozens of people gathered round the scaffold! I was shaking with nerves, I can tell you. 'Would you mind putting your head on the block?' I asked her, ever so polite, just the way you taught me.

Blow me, but the old woman said, 'No! A traitor would put their head on the block, but I'm not a traitor, so I won't!'

Her two guards grabbed her and held her down on her knees. But she was struggling all the time. They couldn't hold her head down because I'd have cut their hands off. That meant she could still move her head around. Then she looked up at me and said, 'Catch me if you can.' She started bobbing and weaving and I started chopping. Well, I made a right mess of her shoulders before I finally got her in the neck and finished her off.

It was my job to hold up the head and cry, 'Behold the head of a traitor!' I was that scared I think I said, 'Behold the head of a tater!' The witnesses were booing and throwing things at me. It was awful, Mum.

But Robert's back now and I'm getting extra lessons. In the meantime I'm working away in the torture chamber. They don't mind if you're clumsy in there and you don't have a big audience.

Give my love to the kids and the cat. I'll be home next week to help with chopping the firewood.

Love,
    Your little Georgie

We don't know what happened to the boy executioner – but his master, Cratwell, was later hanged for robbery!

Of course the good news is that Henry VIII died of a slow disease. His legs had ulcers – open sores that had to be bandaged to stop them dripping all over the place. The Countess of Salisbury's death was messy … but Henry's was long, slow and painful. It's hard to feel sorry for him.

Cardinal John Fisher – June 1535

If you had the power of a king, would you send your dear old teacher for the chop? (On second thoughts, you'd better not answer that!)

Henry VIII's old teacher was called John Fisher. Henry's mother had put Prince Henry in Fisher's special care. But, when the old teacher disagreed with Henry's plans for the Church, Henry ordered the old man's imprisonment.

Some prisoners lived in comfort, but John Fisher spent winter in the Tower of London with just a handful of rags to cover him. In spring, just when he was beginning to warm up, Henry ordered his teacher's death. When Fisher walked to the block he staggered because he was so weak from hunger.

Still, witnesses said he was eager to meet his death and he dressed for what he described as his 'wedding day'.

The Pope had made Fisher a 'cardinal' while the old man was in prison. Henry was furious...

I will send your head to Rome so the Pope can put your cardinal's hat on you himself.

Henry never carried out that threat.

Fisher didn't give the executioner any trouble, but his body was left almost naked for a whole day while the head was stuck on a spike over London Bridge.

Spanish visitors said the heads of traitors over the bridge turned black but Fisher's stayed fresh – this proved he was a saint, they said. It would be interesting to see if it was still fresh today, but you can't. Not only is the old London Bridge gone, but a friend of Fisher's climbed up to the top of the bridge tower one night to pinch the head and give it a proper burial.

Fisher was 66 years old. He was hardly a Tudor terrorist who needed putting to death for Henry's safety.

The Carthusian monks – May 1535

A 'terrorist' is someone who tries to terrify people into doing what they want. So Henry VIII was a terrorist. It wasn't enough to have his enemies locked away or even executed. He had to make an *example* of them.

Three monks from the Carthusian order opposed Henry and were sentenced to be drawn, hanged and quartered. That is, *drawn* feet-first to the scaffold on a sledge, *hanged* till half-dead, taken down and cut open so their guts could be burned on a fire, then beheaded and *quartered*.[1]

1 Some historians describe this punishment for treason as 'hung, drawn and quartered' where 'drawn' means having the bowels drawn from the body. Not that you'd be too worried about getting the words right if it happened to you!

Then, to strike terror into the hearts of their supporters, the severed arm of one monk was nailed to the door of his monastery.

Another Carthusian, Sebastian Newdigate, had been a friend of Henry's and they'd gone hunting together. Henry made an example of him by placing him in a London street, loaded down with chains and lead weights so he couldn't move or even stand up. (Worse ... he couldn't go to the toilet!) He was left, in his own filth, with no food or water until he died. The message was as clear as ever...

Anne Boleyn – 1536

All the school history books will tell you that Henry had wanted a divorce from his first wife, Catherine of Aragon. When the Catholic Church refused to give him a divorce, he scrapped the Catholic Church, made his own church and gave himself a divorce.

Catholics who objected were ruthlessly punished. Even Catherine and Henry's own daughter, Mary Tudor, was locked up for protesting. (New wife Anne didn't like Mary much anyway.) And all for what? Nothing! Because the divorce was pointless when Catherine of Aragon died in 1536 anyway. (There are stories that Anne Boleyn had Catherine poisoned with a delivery of Welsh beer to her castle-prison. That's unlikely.)

One of Henry's best friends, Sir Thomas More, was executed for sticking to his Catholic religion. But, before he died, he said something very wise…

> *Anne Boleyn might strike our heads off like footballs, but it won't be long before her head will dance the same dance!*

(It makes you wonder *where* Thomas More had ever seen a dancing football, but that's beside the point.)

More was *right*. Henry grew fed up with Anne when she failed to give him a son. He had her executed for flirting with other men.

What the school history books don't tell you is how *kind* old Henry was when it came to Anne's execution. He didn't want any of that hacking about and sawing at necks. He sent for a real expert. A swordsman.

Anne Boleyn never laid her neck on a block. She walked into the execution room, said a few words of farewell and was blindfolded. The swordsman didn't want her turned towards him so he said…

Clean off, first time. (Unlike a French swordsman, who took 29 swings of the sword to execute the Count of Chalais in 1626!)

Hundreds of years later there were ghost stories of Anne wandering round the Tower with her head tucked underneath her arm. But there were different ghost stories told at the time of the execution. They said...

- Candles around the tomb of Catherine of Aragon, Anne's enemy, burst into flame the day before the execution. As the blow fell on Anne's neck the next day, the candles went out just as mysteriously. (It could have been the draught from the sword! But, as Catherine was buried 92 miles away in Peterborough, it's a bit unlikely.)

- As Anne died, people reported seeing hares running across the fields – a hare was the sign of a witch, and Anne was suspected of witchcraft. Every year, on the anniversary of the execution on 19 May, hares were seen. Perhaps they still are!

Robert Aske – 1537
In 1536, Henry VIII had created his Church of England but not everyone was happy. In fact, some were ready to revolt. Henry's new laws said...

TO THE PEOPLE OF ENGLAND
In the name of His Most Royal Majesty, King Henry VIII, defender of the faith, the following laws have been enacted...

- All monasteries will close and their wealth transferred to the king and their lands sold.
- The Catholic religion will be replaced by the Protestant religion. There will be an end to the worship of images and all Catholic shrines and books must be destroyed.
- All children must be christened as Protestants. There will be a charge for christenings, marriages and burials
- There will be new taxes on all subjects and no one may eat white bread in future unless a tax is paid to the king

Signed

Thomas Cromwell

Chief minister

THAT'S NOT FAIR! I'M REVOLTING!

HE ALWAYS HAS BEEN

The changes were unpopular, especially in the north of England which had never been too keen on taking orders from rulers in the south.

Riots broke out in Lincoln. The rioters made their own demands...

Henry had a bit of a problem because he had no army ready to crush the riots. Eventually the Duke of Suffolk raised an army and the Lincoln rebels began to go home.

But a new protest, led by the very religious Catholic, Robert Aske, broke out in Pontefract in the north. (Aske had only one eye. Is this why he didn't see eye to eye with Henry?) Aske's protestors called themselves the 'Pilgrimage of Grace'.

These pilgrims carried banners and wore badges that showed the bleeding wounds of Christ – but they weren't bloodthirsty. In fact they were ordinary men and women who wanted to make a peaceful protest.

The Duke of Suffolk had no men to spare to attack Aske because he was too busy in Lincoln. Henry was in desperate trouble.

Only one man could save Henry! And he *did*. That man was

… Robert Aske! Aske said he was not a rebel and he didn't want to destroy Henry. He made his own declaration…

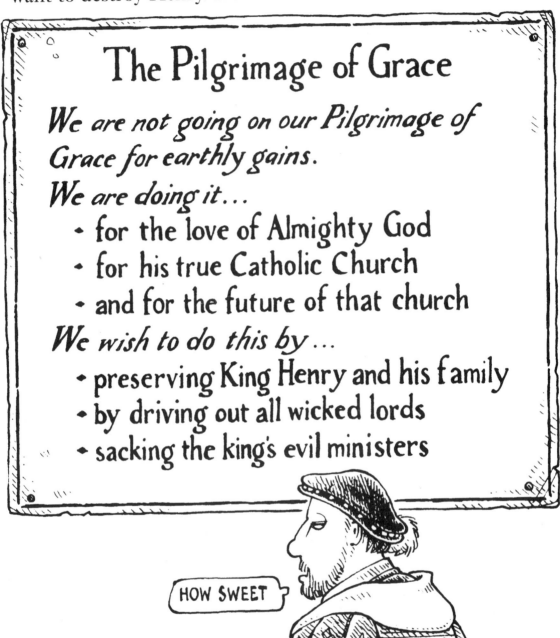

Aske's pilgrims wanted to march south to London to force Henry to give in. Aske refused to let them, saying they were a holy group and not a rioting mob.

What could Henry do? He needed time to get a new army together.

So he told Aske a whopping great fib. He said, more or less…

LOOK, LADS, YOU GO HOME PEACEFULLY AND I'LL LOOK AT YOUR COMPLAINTS. I WILL ALSO PARDON YOU... AS LONG AS YOU MAKE NO MORE TROUBLE

Then he gathered his forces. Some peasants in Cumberland marched on Carlisle and said they were part of the 'Pilgrimage of Grace' (though they weren't). That was just the excuse Henry had been waiting for.

ASKE HAS ASKED FOR IT!

Henry sent in his new army and attacked ruthlessly. Places like Sawley monastery had been reopened by the Pilgrims – Henry's men took the monks and hanged them from the steeple of the church so everyone could see what happened to rebels.

Aske was executed in front of the people who had followed

167

him. Hundreds of his supporters were hanged and a woman was even burned.

So much for Henry's promises.

Did you know...?

It was against the law to foretell the death of a monarch. Anyone who said, 'The king is going to die,' would be executed. Henry VIII fell ill with a fever in 1547 and his doctors knew he was going to die. But they didn't dare *tell* him he was going to die because they'd have been breaking the law and they could have been hanged!

So Henry slipped off to sleep, thinking he was going to live. He must have been really disappointed when he woke up dead.

He was 55 years old and the throne passed to his nine-year-old son Edward VI. (Of course the pretender, Lambert Simnel, had been crowned Edward VI 60 years before. So Henry's son was really Edward the sixth the second.)

Fat Hen

Henry VIII is famous for his huge feasts and his belt-busting eating habits. But what do you know about the Tudors and their tastes? Try this quick quiz and strain your brain! (Or challenge your friends to a competition – see who can score the most – but don't forget to cheat and look at the answers. After all, this is a Horrible History book and it is not suitable for honest, fair and truthful readers.)

1 What would Tudor magistrates do with a merchant who added sawdust to his peppers and spices?

a) Make him eat a plate filled with the spicy-sawdust mix.

b) Lock his head in a pillory and burn the spices under his nose.

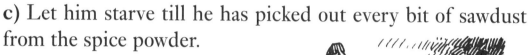

c) Let him starve till he has picked out every bit of sawdust from the spice powder.

2 In 1502, the first European to taste chocolate hated it. Who was it?

a) Christopher Columbus.

b) Henry VIII (when he was an 11-year-old prince).

c) Henry VII's pet dog who pinched it from the palace kitchen and was sick.

3 In 1500 the first cookery book was published in the English language. What was it called?

a) *The Two Fat Lardies*

b) *Filling Feasts for 1500*

c) *The Boke of Cokery*

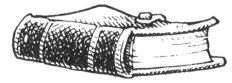

4 Pork and chicken could be served together. How?

a) The back half of a cooked pig was sewn onto the front half of a cockerel.

b) Pork and chicken were minced together into 'chork sausages'.

c) A pig was fed on chicken meat, killed, cooked and served.

5 Kitchen workers in great houses got special treats to add to their wages. Which of the following was often included?

a) Leftover food.

b) Sheep's eyes to take home for their family suppers.

c) Grease scraped from the bottom of the pot when meat has been boiled.

6 Beer was often warmed up and drunk with what dropped in?

a) Frog-spawn.

b) Toast.

c) A silver coin for luck.

7 King Henry VIII treated his wife, Catherine of Aragon, cruelly by giving her a gift of what?

a) Old wine.

b) New wine.

c) A cup of tea.

8 How would you have eaten 'stockfish' in Tudor times?

a) Skinned, gutted and eaten raw.

b) Battered with chips.

c) Battered with a hammer.

9 Who was the 'Queen of the Pea'?

a) The lavatory cleaner.

b) Anne Boleyn because she had pea-green sleeves.

c) A woman who found a pea in her Christmas cake.

10 How would Henry VIII have eaten his meat?

a) Carved a piece from the bone, dipped it in a sauce and put it in his mouth.

b) Chewed the meat from the bone and thrown the bone to his dogs.

c) Torn the meat with his bare hands, stuffed it in his mouth and wiped his hands on his tunic.

Answers:

1b) In 1493 the London Grocers' Company employed men whose job it was to check spices as they came into the port. Merchants had been adding gravel to peppercorns and nutmeg and other spices. These checkers were known as 'garbellers' – not to be confused with history teachers who rush through lessons. They are garblers, but they probably won't set fire to pepper under your nose.

2a) Columbus had discovered America in 1492. Ten years later he was visiting the Gulf of Honduras when

171

natives offered him a drink of *xocoatl* (pronounced *chocoatl*). It was mixed with honey and spices and served cold and frosty. Columbus drank it politely but said, 'Yeuch!' Still, he brought some beans back to Europe and now it's a billion-pound industry. Hands up if you though chocolate bars came from Mars?

3c) 'Cokery' was just the Tudor way of writing cookery – it had nothing to do with drinking Coke … or eating lumps of coke for that matter. Don't you learn some amazing things from this boke?

BLIMEY! DOES THAT MEAN US BLOKES ARE REALLY BLOOKS?

4a) Cooks often sewed two creatures together to make an entertaining meal. The front of a chicken and back of a pig stitched together made the legendary creature, the 'cockatrice'. They also served a pig's stomach stuffed with minced pork and spices, then covered with almonds to look like a hedgehog. (If you're really stupid you could sew the front of a jeep on to the back of a dog to try to get a Land Rover.) Vegetables were also carved into fantastic shapes of birds and animals. Would you enjoy a carrot parrot?

Baked potumpkin

5c) You too could have some nice grease if you worked hard. You may also get rabbit skins (after the angry rabbits had been cooked and became hot cross bunnies). You could also have free clothes and good shoes. But you couldn't have leftover food scraps. They had to be given to the poor. But if a joint of meat or a pie had not been touched then it belonged to the person who served it!

I DON'T WANT TO PUT YOU OFF, M'LADY, BUT THAT PIE'S NOT VERY NICE

6b) Warm beer with toast dropped in! Urgh! But it was better than some of the other things stirred in to give it a bit of flavour … like raw egg! And a popular Tudor Christmas drink (that you may like to leave for Santa Claus instead of a glass of sherry) was called 'lambswool'. This was hot beer with roasted apple pieces, nutmeg, ginger and sugar. When it was whipped up, the scum (sorry, *froth*) on the top looked like lambs' wool.

EGG AND TOAST? SOUNDS MORE LIKE BREAKFAST

7b) Catherine was ill and wanted some old Spanish wine to soothe her aches. Henry ordered new wine to be sent to her – in Tudor times this would make a sick person worse, and Fat Hen knew this. A kind servant sent Catherine the old wine that she wanted. When Henry found out, the servant was sacked. The old wine gift had given Henry a new whine.

8c) Stockfish was dried fish and it was hard as a history teacher's heart! You had to batter it with a wooden hammer and soak it in water for two hours before you could chew it. So strike a pike, clout a trout, pound a flounder or bludgeon a gudgeon … but be careful not to get flat fishy fingers.

9c) On the 12th night after Christmas (6 January if you haven't got a calendar) many houses celebrated by baking a fruit cake. A pea (or a bean) was baked into the cake. The person who found it became the King or Queen of the Pea (or Bean). They sat at the head of the table and got the best food, but had to entertain all the guests.

10a) Shocking but true. Henry is often pictured as eating like an animal with grease dripping down his beard and servants ducking the bare bones as he threw them over his shoulder. But he was a great prince who would eat in the correct Tudor manner: carved pieces of meat dipped in sauces and placed in the mouth. Cats and dogs were banned from the dining rooms and clothes were far too fine and expensive to have greasy hands wiped over them. Hands would be washed in rose water and dried on linen napkins. Of course, Henry ate huge amounts, but he didn't have the manners of a pig as most people seem to think. (He'd have been shocked to see the average school dinner hall at lunchtime!)

Little Ed

1547 Edward VI, Tudor the third, takes the throne. He is a Catholic-hating young man. He is also God-fearing, which is just as well because he'll be meeting him soon.

1553 Weedy Ed dies at the age of 15. It's party time for the Catholics. No more Tudor kings … ever!

King Edward VI (reigned 1547–1553)

Henry VIII had waited 28 years for a son and at last Edward was born. Ed's mother, Jane Seymour, died after giving birth, which was very thoughtless of her. Henry wasn't going to lose baby Ed, so he tried to make sure he was properly cared for. If cotton wool had been invented then, Henry would have wrapped his son in the stuff.

Did you know…?

1 The floors and walls of Edward's rooms were washed down three times every day to keep him free from disease. No wonder he grew up a bit wet!

2 Although Edward was precious to his father, Henry hardly ever visited him or read the reports the servants sent him.

3 Edward was raised by nurses because his mother died when he was just a few days old. But his chief nurse was called 'Mother Jack'. That must have confused him a bit. But it is no excuse for the ancient historical joke...

4 Edward took everything very seriously. His teachers thought he was wonderful and very good at history. The trouble was he had no sense of humour. It was reported that he only laughed out loud once in his life! Maybe his teachers should have given him a Horrible History book to read!

5 King Henry sent the sons of his favourite lords to do lessons with Edward so the boy wouldn't grow up alone. But it was a dangerous job being a schoolmate of Little Ed. Once Edward's friends persuaded him to swear 'thunderous oaths' like Henry VIII. Edward did this and was told off. But his friends were given a whipping.

6 Little Ed may have grown up to be a Big Ed … and almost certainly a big-*head* too! His teacher, John Cheke, fell ill. Edward told everyone, 'He will be all right. This morning I prayed for him and God will answer my prayer.' Would *you* pray for *your* teacher to get better?

7 Edward also had his father's terrible Tudor cruelty. In a fit of temper he once took a falcon and pulled out all its feathers one by one. He then ripped it into four pieces and threatened that he would do the same to his teachers. (Teachers probably deserve to be torn into four pieces … but you wouldn't hurt a poor little falcon, would you?)

8 Edward died a painful death from a lung disease known as 'consumption'. The Duke of Northumberland was Edward's protector (a protector ran the country when the monarch was too young to do it). He wanted to keep Ed alive as long as possible – or long enough for Ed change his will and name Lady Jane Grey as the next queen. So Northumberland sacked Edward's doctors and employed a 'wise woman'.

The special potion she fed the dying King contained the poison arsenic. It kept him alive … but in agony at the same time. Ed was in so much pain he was praying to God to let him kick the bucket. Once Ed had changed his will, Northumberland was ready to let Edward die. The protector sacked the wise woman and called the royal doctors back. There is even a story that Northumberland had the wise woman murdered. But that's daft. If she was a *wise* woman she'd have seen it coming and escaped!

9 The people of London heard that Edward was dead – or dying. They marched to Greenwich Palace and said…

Edward's attendants knew the dying King was too weak to go out and meet them so they said…

So Northumberland ordered the attendants to lift Ed out of bed, carry him to the window and prop him up so the people could see their king. The plan didn't work all that well because the people were shocked by what they saw. Ed's skinny body was swollen, his fingers were turning black and dropping off. His hair had fallen out. He looked like something the attendants had dug out of the graveyard.

10 The common people were sure that Northumberland was trying to poison Edward. (Which he was!) Northumberland said it was Mary Tudor's fault. He said that last time Mary visited her brother she cast an evil spell over him…

> *She overlooked him with the evil eye of witchcraft!*

Mary was popular at that time. No one believed Northumberland. He was going to be in trouble if Mary ever took the throne.

Daft doctors

Edward VI's doctors made one last attempt to save Ed's life. If you ever get consumption like Little Ed then take antibiotics – or take a plastic bag to collect your fingers and toes when they drop off – but *do not* take what Ed's doctors gave him…

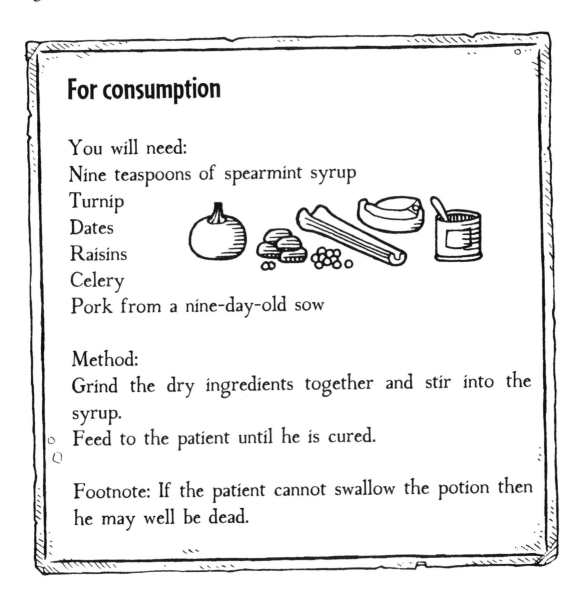

For consumption

You will need:
Nine teaspoons of spearmint syrup
Turnip
Dates
Raisins
Celery
Pork from a nine-day-old sow

Method:
Grind the dry ingredients together and stir into the syrup.
Feed to the patient until he is cured.

Footnote: If the patient cannot swallow the potion then he may well be dead.

Of course, if you *really* want a flavour of this miserable medicine you could try eating a stick of celery dipped in spearmint flavouring … but anyone with half a brain cell would be happy just to imagine the taste.

No wonder Edward VI's minister, William Cecil, said…

God protect us from doctors.

Just to add a final gruesome touch to Ed's death, a sudden summer storm sprang up. Lightning flashed, thunder crashed … and hailstones as red as fresh blood rained down. 'Henry VIII wanted Mary to be queen,' the people said. 'Northumberland is trying to get Lady Jane Grey on the throne. Henry has risen from the grave! This storm has been sent by Henry to show his anger!'

Ed died.

The curious case of the corpse

Edward VI's grave is in Westminster Abbey. But is his body buried there? There is a strange story that dead Ed was not the corpse in the coffin.

Here is a story that you may or may not believe…

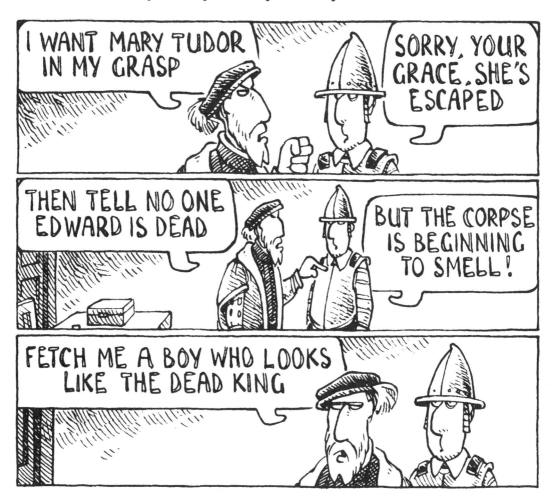

Northumberland's agents found a young man who looked a bit like Edward...

So, the story goes, a substitute corpse is buried in Westminster Abbey. The real Edward VI is somewhere in the grounds of Greenwich Palace.

Is this gory story true? Here's a clue.

The body that was supposed to be Edward's was preserved, laid in an open coffin and taken to the Abbey. Twelve lords took it in turns to guard the coffin before the day of the funeral. This was quite usual.

BUT ... a shocked visitor from France wrote that the 12 lords watched over the coffin 'without torches or tapers'.

Imagine that – babysitting a corpse *in the dark*!

Why? Work it out for yourself.

The kiss of death

Edward was still just 15 when he fell seriously ill so the country was controlled by a 'protector', the Duke of Northumberland. The Duke had a great idea…

> YOU CAN'T LEAVE THE CROWN TO YOUR CATHOLIC SISTER MARY - YOU HATE CATHOLICS. WHY NOT LEAVE IT TO LADY JANE GREY - SHE'S A GOOD PROTESTANT

> LADY JANE IS MARRIED TO YOUR SON, ISN'T SHE?

> OH! SILLY ME! I'D FORGOTTEN! NEVER MIND, SHE'LL MAKE A GREAT QUEEN

Ed died and Jane was proclaimed queen. Angry Mary marched in and had her arrested. Jane was queen for just nine days and was arrested when she was just 15 years old. She saw her 16th birthday … but not her 17th. Mary had her executed.

Edward VI left Jane Grey the crown though she never got to wear it. It would have been kinder if he'd left her a bottle of his poisonous medicine.

Misery Mary

1553 Mary I, Tudor four, takes the throne. She's even more miserable than little brother Ed was. She is also a devout Catholic. The English people don't know if they're coming or going with this religious yo-yo.

1554 Mary marries King Philip of Spain. She marries for love, he marries to get his paws on the English crown. When he doesn't get it, he goes home in a huff. He'll be back … with a few thousand troops and an armada.

1558 Now Mary dies. She's lasted even less time than little brother Ed! Three Tudor funerals in 11 years and the family are hopping the twig like budgerigars. New Protestant queen, Mary's half-sister Elizabeth, will stay on her royal perch a lot longer.

Queen Mary I (reigned 1553–1558)

Mary was a misery. Her dad had divorced her mum, Catherine of Aragon, to marry Anne Boleyn. When Mary tried to fight for Catherine, Henry had her shut up in some miserable and uncomfortable houses. But, before he died, he said Mary could be queen if Edward died without children.

Of course Edward did die. But Ed's chief minister, the

Duke of Northumberland, wasn't going to give up his power that easily. He plonked little Jane Grey on the throne, put one of his sons on the throne beside her and sent another of his sons to capture Mary.

Mary knew the English people would not be happy with a Catholic queen. When some Protestants from Cambridge found that she had spent the night in a nearby house they burned the house down!

So how could Mary win the support of the Protestants?

a) Tell the English they would be Catholic whether they liked it or not.

b) Give up her Catholic religion.

c) Lie. Tell the English the country would stay Protestant then change it when she became queen.

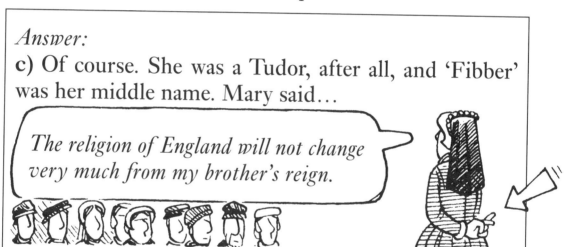

Answer:

c) Of course. She was a Tudor, after all, and 'Fibber' was her middle name. Mary said…

The religion of England will not change very much from my brother's reign.

It worked. (The Tudor people hadn't yet learned the lesson, 'Never trust a Tudor.') Gentlemen and peasants made an army of 15,000 to march on London in support of Mary. The Duke of Northumberland marched out to meet Mary's army. And what did the Londoners do as soon as Northumberland left? Rebelled, of course, and offered their support to Mary.

In London they celebrated by…

They were pleased. They sent a letter to Mary that said…

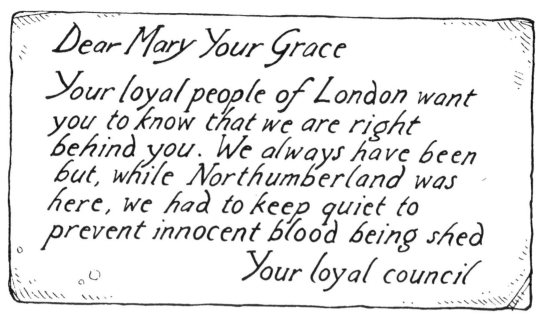

Dear Mary Your Grace

Your loyal people of London want
you to know that we are right
behind you. We always have been
but, while Northumberland was
here, we had to keep quiet to
prevent innocent blood being shed

Your loyal council

Ho! Ho! A likely story. But Mary was happy enough to accept their offer of support.

Even little Jane Grey said she was happy. She said…

I am very glad I am no longer queen.

She wasn't throwing her cap in the air but, in a few months' time, she'd be able to throw her head in the air … but not catch it.

And those bonfires would be lit under Protestants when Mary broke her promise to them.

Cruel cuts

The Duke of Northumberland was in Cambridge when he heard that Londoners had deserted him and Jane Grey. What could he do? He went into the market square with a cap full of gold coins. He threw the cap in the air, scattering the coins while he declared, 'God save Queen Mary!' While the people scrambled for the coins, his friends noticed that Northumberland was crying.

Meanwhile his servants ripped his badge off their coats and sneaked off home. They weren't going to hang around with a loser – or they might find themselves hanging around from a gallows! Northumberland was taken to the Tower of London. The mob threw mud, horse droppings (and human droppings!) at him as he was led through the streets.

Mary made another one of those treacherous Tudor promises...

I will spare the life of Lady Jane Grey.

Northumberland was the first to go. The judges passed sentence. He was guilty of treason so he was to be hanged, drawn and quartered. They added the tasty little line...

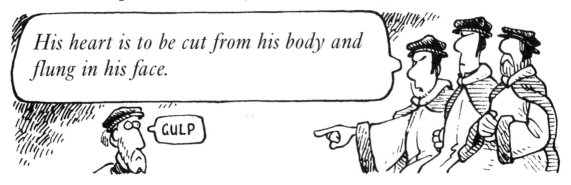

His heart is to be cut from his body and flung in his face.

GULP

Northumberland tried every trick in the book to avoid execution. He tried weeping and pleading...

PLEASE DON'T KILL ME... GROVEL-CREEP. MY MUMMY WOULD BE SO UPSET!

188

Then he tried the old Tudor trick – lying…

ACTUALLY, I HAVE ALWAYS BEEN A GOOD CATHOLIC, GROVEL-CREEP. YOU WOULDN'T KILL A CATHOLIC, WOULD YOU?

A couple of weeks later he climbed onto the scaffold watched by 10,000 people who hated his guts. He made a final speech in which he admitted…

I have deserved a thousand deaths.

But he only got one.

Then it was Lady Jane Grey's turn. She was told she would stand trial and be found guilty, but not to worry, Queen Mary would spare her life. Fifteen-year-old Jane was pleased and said, 'She is a merciful queen!' Jane Grey had Tudor blood herself – so she should have known better!

But a Protestant rebel, Sir Thomas Wyatt, spoiled it all for her. Wyatt led a group of armed men from Kent towards London. He said he wanted to put Lady Jane on the throne. The rebellion failed.

Mary and her ministers decided that the best way to stop any more rebellions like that was to execute Jane and her husband.

At least Jane didn't grovel like her father-in-law, Northumberland. Instead she said…

I am ready and glad to end my woeful days.

It's strange that the two Tudor women to die on the block (Jane Grey and Mary Queen of Scots, 30 years later), both died bravely. Jane's father-in-law had begged for his life, her father pleaded for mercy and her husband was 'in a state of collapse, weeping and angry about his unkind fate'. He was still sobbing when his head was lopped off the next day.

Jane followed him to a scaffold and acted out a scene that would have been comical if it hadn't been so gruesome. The executioner showed her the block. She knelt down and tied a handkerchief over her own eyes. But, once she was blindfolded she couldn't remember where the block was. She waved her hands about wildly calling, 'What shall I do? Where is it?'

After an agonizing wait someone guided her hands to the block and she laid her neck on it. She died bravely. Tudor women were tough.

Foul fairs

Mary was quite popular with the people of England even though she was a Catholic. You see, the Catholics had lots of saints and every saint had their special day in the calendar, and a lot of those days were *holidays*. In the Middle Ages as many as one day in every three was a saint's day. How would you like that? Two days' work, one day off, two days' work, one day off.

The Protestants had put a stop to a lot of this saints nonsense. But there were some holidays they didn't change. The days when great fairs were held.

Forget swings, roundabouts and roller-coasters. Tudor fairs were large markets and they were dirty, dangerous and disgusting places. You'd have loved the noise, the plays and the games – but hated the cruelty to animals.

In London, the greatest fair was Saint Bartholomew's Day fair. In the Middle Ages it had been a 'cloth fair'. By Tudor times there was more fun and food and fighting than cloth! The Victorians were so disgusted by it, they finally closed it down. They *would*.

In Nottingham, a great goose fair started before 1540. It went on for three weeks and 20,000 geese were sold. If you've ever seen one goose's droppings then you can just about imagine the mess left by 20,000 of them!

GOOSE POO! GOOSE POO! GET YOUR GOOSE POO HERE. GREAT FOR THE GARDEN! TWO GROATS A BAG!

Farmers had to walk the geese to market. Sometimes they travelled for weeks. The geese were given 'shoes' of tar and sand to stop their feet from being hurt.

Not just geese were sold, but lace and cheese and willow baskets.[1] But some fairs, like Birmingham and Enfield, were mostly for selling gingerbread.

Terrible Tudor things to do on school sports day
Rope walking

At Tudor fairs a popular entertainment was to watch 'rope walkers' – men and girls who climbed on to a rope high above the ground and danced or juggled. The ropes were slack (not like a modern circus tightrope walker's) so this was a difficult trick.

Edward VI enjoyed watching one particular rope walker who attached one end of the rope to the battlements of a castle and the other end to the ground. The man then walked down to the ground without falling into the moat.

1. A carnival is still held in Nottingham on the first weekend of October. Now it has changed to become a fun fair.

You never see that these days. What a good idea for school sports day! Why not sponsor your head teacher to attempt it from the school roof to the field or yard below?

Flea circus

Another sad fairground loss is the flea circus. Fleas were trained to perform circus acts. They needed a trainer (to keep them up to scratch).

Flea circuses were still popular in this century but have disappeared. Why are you unlikely to see this attraction at your school fete?

a) They are banned by the Society Against Nastiness To Animals (SANTA).

b) Fleas have become rare since the invention of the vacuum cleaner.

c) Modern fleas are not as obedient as Tudor fleas and refuse to do tricks.

Answer:

b) The invention of the vacuum has done terrible harm to flea populations in the modern world. Cute tigers and cuddly rhinos are called 'endangered species' and are protected. Who protects the poor little flea? No one! After all the flea has done for humanity! If it wasn't for the flea we wouldn't have had the Black Death and other exciting bits of horrible history. It's about time the Society Against Flea Extermination (SAFE) jumped into action before it's too late.

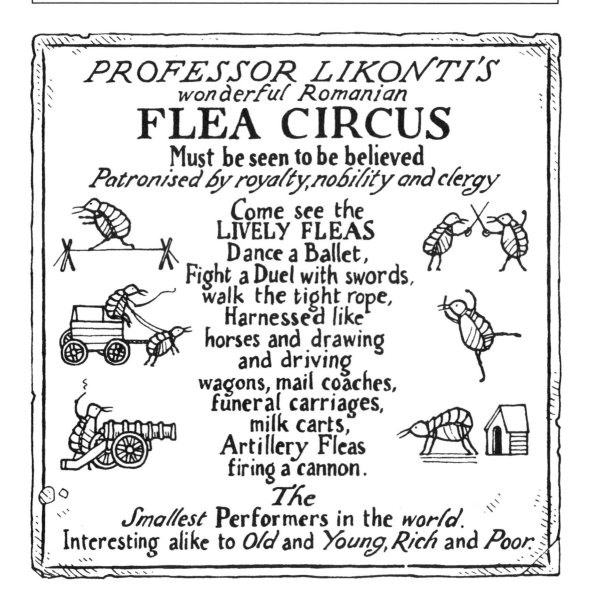

Beware the fair

Fairs were popular places for pickpockets and cutpurses. Some criminals paid a boy to climb up a nearby church steeple. The pickpocket would cry, 'My God! Look at that!' While the crowds looked up at the boy on the steeple, the pickpocket would go through the crowd and empty their purses.

Naughty knights

When a king was crowned he usually knighted several young gentlemen. They were called Knights of the Order of the Bath – an honour invented in the reign of Henry IV (reigned 1399–1413). They took their name from the curious old ceremony that went with the knighting.

The ~~New~~ *Nude* King's Order of the Bath

1 First, take a large tub and fill it with warm ~~water.~~ *sticky pudding and custard*

2 The King takes off all his clothes and ~~climbs~~ in. *dives*

3 The knights take off all their clothes and ~~climb in with him.~~ *run around the castle*

4 Each knight takes a turn at kissing the King on his bare ~~shoulder.~~ *BUM!*

5 All climb out and have a jolly good rub down with a ~~warm towel~~ *Hedgehog*

Mary Tudor was the first queen England had crowned. (Empress Matilda had never been crowned when she fought to rule England 400 years before.)

Would you believe it? Mary did not want to have a bath with all of her knights! (Clearly she had no sense of fun or adventure.) One of her earls took her place in the tub.

Phil death us do part
Philip I of Spain (reigned 1527–1598)

Misery Mary's big mistake was to marry Philip of Spain in 1554. He was as popular as a piranha in a goldfish bowl. The English didn't like him because he was Spanish *and* he was Catholic … and Spanish Catholics were 'saving' the souls of Protestants by torturing them and burning their bodies.

What happened was the Church found the victims guilty and handed them over to the government. The *government* burned them. Philip was right – the Catholic Church *didn't* burn a single person. But they sent thousands to their deaths. Phil brought this charming little hobby to England.

Mary and Philip were engaged before they had even met. Mary loved her young husband madly. He was never quite so keen. As some of his unkind (but honest) courtiers said when they arrived for the wedding…

Mary is older than we have been told. She is not at all beautiful and is small and flabby rather than fat. She has a white complexion, is fair and has no eyebrows.

She has lost most of her teeth.

She dresses very badly.

Cruellest of all was the courtier who said…

What shall the King do with such an old bitch?

What *did* Philip do?

I'M OFF TO FLANDERS TO FIGHT FOR SPAIN. I'LL BE BACK IN SIX WEEKS

He lied, of course. He came back over a year later for a short stay then left for good. Mary was very miserable. And every time she got miserable she decided she must have upset God. So, to make God happy, she burned more and more heretics.

A miserable Mary was a murderous Mary.

Did you know…?
Mary was so desperate to get Philip back to England that she ordered her cooks to send his favourite meat pies across to Flanders. 'The way to a man's heart is through his stomach,' they used to say. But the way to Philip's heart was not through meat pies and he didn't return.

Hell for heretics

Mary believed that people who didn't follow the Catholic ways would roast in front of the fires of hell. These people were called 'heretics'. They had to repent (say, 'Sorry, God!') before they died. The best way to make them say 'Sorry' was to stick them on a bonfire; once they had a feel for hell-fire they would repent.

The fire would not be put out, of course. They would die whether they repented or not! But at least Mary felt sure they would go to heaven and the pain would be worthwhile.

Mary's Spanish marriage was unpopular with the English people. When the burnings started they began to *really* hate her.

HERETIC HOOPER'S HORROR

Today the Bishop of Gloucester, John Hooper, died horribly at the stake. He is the second victim of Queen Mary's cruel Catholic campaign. When the Queen signed his death warrant she said clearly, 'Don't try to make yourself a martyr!' But that's what he'll become after the dreadful death in Gloucester.

Hooper had a bag of gunpowder placed around his neck but it failed to explode and give him a merciful death. Instead he suffered for three-quarters of an hour, begging the spectators to fan the flames and speed the end.

One appalled spectator (who does not wish to be named) said, 'I blame the Spaniard, Philip. The sooner Mary dies and leaves the throne to Princess Elizabeth the happier we'll all be.'

The bungled execution follows the death of John Rogers in London last week. The condemned man was not even allowed to say goodbye to his wife and children. An angry crowd protested about this added cruelty. Throughout the country hundreds are being whipped in the stocks for speaking out against Queen Mary.

A woman (who does not wish to give her name) said, 'When the Queen was crowned I cheered with the rest of them. She said she'd forget that Catholic nonsense. We were cheated.' The ashes of Hooper's fire are growing cool here in Gloucester, but the fire of anger against the Queen and her husband is burning hot and strong across the land.

Mary's cousin, Cardinal Reginald Pole, came back from Rome to help her change England back to a Catholic country. (You may remember his mum, Margaret Pole, Countess of Salisbury, who had her old head hacked off by Henry.) Reggie Pole was practically running the country for Mary.

While Mary was burning living Protestants, Reggie preferred digging up the corpses of dead heretics and burning them instead. (This does not make a lot of sense if the idea was for them to repent before they died!)

The law said that Mary had to sign every heretic's death warrant. She must have had writer's cramp because there were a lot – 240 men and 60 women. Some were popular preachers; some were simple peasants whose only crime was that they couldn't recite the Lord's Prayer.

A rebel leader called Cleobury went around East Anglia proclaiming that Mary was dead and Elizabeth should become queen. Few people supported him and he was arrested. When he was questioned it turned out that he was a Protestant and a convicted burglar. He gave up his job to lead the rebellion. What job? When he wasn't burgling houses, he was a schoolteacher! He was hanged (for being a rebel, not for being a teacher).

Flaming Mary

Some modern historians think Mary has been treated unfairly in history books. 'She wasn't all that bad,' they say. In terms of executing people her father Henry VIII was worse. It's the horrible burnings where she's the top Tudor:

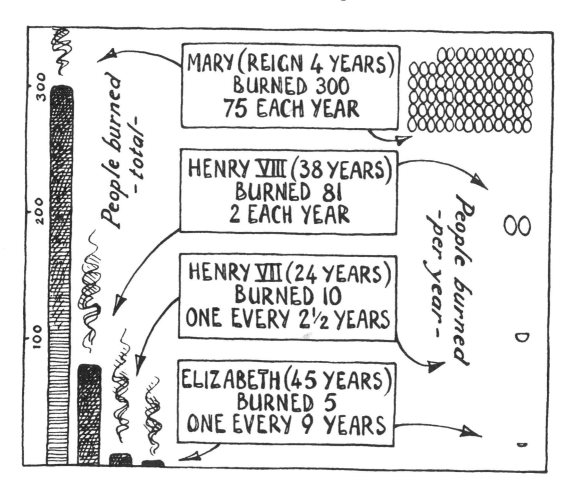

Truesome but gruesome

As Mary lay dying, England and France were at war. Philip's Spain was at war with France so wife Mary's England had to join in ... whether they liked it or not! A peace treaty was brought to Mary for her to sign but she was too ill with influenza to read it. The documents stayed by her bedside. When she died the next day her ministers looked for the papers by the bedside ... but they had vanished.

After searching the room from top to bottom they questioned Mary's chief lady-in-waiting. 'Have you seen any long rolls of parchment?'

'Long rolls of parchment? Oh, yes. They were so useful I used them all up.'

'Used them for what?'

'Why, to wrap up the Queen's corpse!'

SHE'S BEEN TREATED FOR INFLUENZA

Disgusting diseases

If you catch influenza ('flu) you'll probably get a couple of days off school. If you are really ill (or a good actor) you may get a week off school. But Tudor 'flu would make sure you never went back to school again – it could kill you as it killed Queen Mary I.

The Tudors didn't understand about germs. They thought sickness was carried in bad smells – in which case your dad's socks would be a deadly weapon! So it's not surprising there were a lot of terrible Tudor dangers to overcome if you wanted to reach old age ... or even school age. Try this quick quiz to see how much more you understand about illness and disease than your Tudor ancestors...

True or false?

1 The thing that killed most sailors was shipwrecks.

2 Elizabeth I had the disease smallpox and survived.

3 Only prisoners caught 'jail fever'.

4 Henry VII's coronation was delayed because he had 'sweating sickness'.

5 Some Elizabethans believed that going to the theatre was the cause of the plague.

Answers:

1 False. The disease 'scurvy' killed more sailors than shipwrecks, wars at sea and all other diseases put together. When they went on long voyages they hadn't enough fresh fruit and vegetables so they didn't get enough vitamin C. The result was disgusting and you wouldn't want to know ... but here it is anyway. After three months you'd feel tired and have no energy. After five months your skin becomes rough and dry. By six months your legs start to bleed and if you get a wound it won't heal. From seven to eight months your gums go soft, swell up and turn purple. The teeth become loose and old wounds begin to open up.

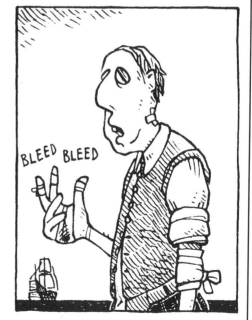

BLEED BLEED

203

If you've had no fresh fruit or veg by nine months you'll have heart and lung problems that can kill you … but you'll feel so rotten that death would make a nice change!

2 True. Elizabeth caught smallpox at the age of 29. This charming disease gives you a high temperature and pains in the head and the muscles. This sometimes ended with the lungs filling with blood and the patient dying. But, if you survived another two to five days, then a rash appeared that grew into great pimples. These burst and the scabs dropped off after a few weeks, but the scars they left behind were

with you for life. This was one reason why Elizabeth wore thick white make-up. Her devoted lady-in-waiting, Lady Sydney, caught the disease from nursing the Queen. Lady Sydney survived but her face was so damaged that she left the royal court and hid herself away for the rest of her life. (Why didn't she just stay and wear a paper bag over her head?)

3 False. 'Jail fever' was a form of the Typhus disease. It arrived in England in 1522 during the reign of Henry VIII. The first outbreak was in Cambridge where it spread from the prisoners to everyone in the courtroom. The jury, the spectators and the judges all caught the fever which also gave them a red rash over their bodies.

More than half of the victims survived but no one understood what caused this dread disease. In fact, it is carried by lice – head lice (nits) and body lice. People in crowded, dirty conditions like ships, armies and jails shared

their lice and the lice carried the germs from one to another. The really, *really*, sad thing is that the poor innocent little lice caught the disease too and they died! They didn't ask to be locked up in a jail with all those filthy humans! (Can't you just picture a tragic louse with a high temperature and a rash? How did it feel? Lousy!)

4 False. It was delayed because many people in London had this plague. 'Sweating sickness' was a Tudor disease which arrived with Henry Tudor at the Battle of Bosworth Field. It's probable that the disease was carried by the soldiers he brought with him from France. Sweating sickness (or 'the sweat') arrived without warning in the morning or at night. Shivering was followed by sweating and then terrible weakness. If your body stopped sweating then you started peeing. If you survived two days then you'd probably live. Many died in the first 24 hours. The good news is that children and wrinklies were spared this disease usually, and so were the poor. It struck more upper class men and, weirdly, seemed to stop at the Borders of Scotland every time it broke out. Maybe the

disease hated the bagpipes!

5 True. In the 1590s the plague spread though Tudor England repeatedly – usually in the summer. London magistrates closed the theatre to stop it spreading. But some religious people believed the theatre *caused* the plague. They said the theatre was wicked and God punished theatre-goers by giving them the plague. What would they have said about television?

Bad Bess

1558 Mary's half-sister Elizabeth takes the throne and, typical Tudor, changes everything around. She tells the English that they are going to be Protestants again.

1587 Queen Bess's cousin, Catholic Mary Queen of Scots, is a menace. She's been thrown out of Scotland and imprisoned in England … but is plotting to break free and murder Bess. The English Queen remembers her father's fast fix for wicked women and has Mary's head lopped off.

1588 Phil's back. The Catholic king of Spain wants his dead wife's throne. He tries to invade with an armada of ships but English navy nobbles him.

1603 Queen Bess, the last Tudor, dies. James, son of Mary Queen of Scots, comes down from Edinburgh to rule. Terrible Tudors terminated. Slimy Stuarts succeed.

Queen Elizabeth I (reigned 1558–1603)

Queen Elizabeth had her father's bad temper and her grandfather's meanness. Both Elizabeth and her big sister

Mary enjoyed playing cards. Mary was a loser, but Elizabeth won a fortune. Why?

Was it because Elizabeth was a skilful player?

No. It was because no one dared to beat her! If she lost, she sulked or lost her temper. It was easier (but expensive) to let Elizabeth win. While most Tudor workers were lucky to earn two or three pounds a year from working, one of Elizabeth's courtiers, Lord North, lost ten pounds *every week* at playing cards with the Queen.[1] He was almost ruined.Here's an Elizabethan card game you may like to try. You can play it against friends – for matchsticks, *not* for money!

Mumchance at cards

You need:
A pack of playing cards.
Two or more players.

To play:
The cards are shuffled and placed face down on a table.
Each player in turn calls the name of a card – everyone has to name a different card. The cards are turned over one at a time. The player whose card is turned over first wins a point.
The first to ten points is the winner.
Advanced play: Do not shuffle the cards each time. Instead place the turned cards to one side. Good players will remember which cards have been turned over and will not name them.

1. Lord North was the Treasurer. His job was to look after England's money. If the Tudors knew the way he lost so much at cards they'd have been very worried! Would you trust that man with your money?

Crafty card sharps

It wasn't only the Queen who took money off people at cards. There were criminals called 'cozeners' who made money out of victims they called 'conies'.

This is how they did it...

Coney catching for a profit

London is full of them! Conies from the countryside with fat purses just waiting to be emptied. Here's how to do it.

You need:
A gold coin.
A few silver shillings.
A partner (your 'barnacle').
A pack of marked cards or a pair of trick dice.

1 First catch your coney. Go to St Paul's Churchyard where all the farm fools gather. Listen for one who speaks with a curious accent. If they say, 'Oooh! Arrrrh!' then you know that he's a coney. Now, drop the gold coin on the ground so that he can't miss it. As he bends to pick it up say, 'Ah! You saw it at the same moment as me. I'll tell you what – let's share it.' With any luck he'll say, 'Oooh! Arrrrh!' then tell him you need to go to a local tavern to change it and offer to buy a drink with your half.

2 Show him a card game and bet a shilling or two. Make sure that he wins about five shillings from you. Then say, 'You're so good you should be playing someone with much more money.' Then point to your barnacle and say, 'That man over there is rich – and stupid. Let's invite him to have a game.' With any luck he'll say, 'Oooh! Arrrrh!'

3 Let the coney win a pile of money from your barnacle. Then raise the stakes till he is betting with all the money in his purse. When all of his money is on the table then make sure he loses. Your barnacle takes the pot of money and shares it with you later. Say, 'Bad luck,' to the coney. He'll probably say, 'Oooh! Arrrrh!'

Other tricks included selling tickets for plays – plays that were never performed! A man called Richard Vennor tried this and pocketed all of the money. But, in the end, he was caught and thrown in prison.

At first, Vennor used his money to buy a private cell, good food and wine from the jailer. But, when the money ran out, he was thrown in 'The Hole' with 50 other men to sleep on bare boards with 50 *other* men, women and children. The cold in winter or the disease in summer or the bad food killed anyone who stayed too long. The poet, Thomas Dekker, said that in The Hole you are 'buried before you are dead'. Richard Vennor died.

Cozening can be bad for your health!

Potty plots

The first Tudor, Henry VII, had many plots against his life to deal with. His granddaughter, Elizabeth I, was no different.

Some of the plots were serious and some were just hoaxes. The Essex rebellion in 1601 was real enough though. Elizabeth had a favourite young courtier, the Earl of Essex. But the trouble started back in 1594, when Elizabeth became annoyed with him. He had to do something to win back her friendship. He came up with the idea of rescuing Elizabeth from a plot against her life.

So Essex wrote to the Queen…

Your Gracious Majesty,

I write with sad and worrying news. My spies (who work for your protection even though they cost me a lot of my own money) have uncovered a plot. It seems they have heard that your doctor, Roderigo Lopez, has been paid by his Spanish masters to poison you.

> *Lopez, as you know, is Jewish. Jews are not popular and you would be most popular if you had him executed. If I have saved your life with this news then I am well rewarded.*
>
> *Your most humble servant*
>
> *Essex*

The Queen took the letter seriously. She then called her own ministers to question all the Spanish spies they could find and uncover the truth.

She was furious … with Essex.

> My Lord Essex,
>
> I have looked into your claims against Doctor Lopez most carefully. It seems the man is innocent. Your spies are fools… and so is their master. Do not bother me with this matter again.
>
> Elizabeth

Essex's plan had gone badly wrong. What could he do?

And that's just what Essex did for two days. Then he had another idea…

Essex had all the people Lopez worked with brought to his dungeons…

But, when the witnesses were faced with torture, they changed their story … wouldn't you?

Elizabeth *had* to believe in the doctor's guilt now. The poor man was sent to the scaffold where he died a traitor's death.

But oh yes, he almost certainly was.

Sadly, Lopez and the witnesses weren't the only victims of the Earl's cruel plot. The English people turned against all the Jews in England, beat them, robbed them and drove them from their homes.

Even the playwright William Shakespeare cashed in on the hatred of Jews by writing a play with a Jewish villain, *The Merchant of Venice*. It was a huge success … except with the suffering Jews, of course.

Essex's end

Not every plot against Elizabeth was so harmless. But the most dangerous one was led by Essex, the man who sent Doctor Lopez to his dreadful death. It served him right that his plot failed and he was executed. He was lucky that he didn't suffer the way Lopez had.

The problem was that the Queen was getting old and feeble. Essex reckoned it was time she handed over the real power to someone young and fit. Someone just like him, in fact.

The rebellion caused a sensation at the time. If there had been newspapers in Elizabeth's day, then the front pages may have looked something like this…

25 Feb. 1601 **Tudor Times** one groat

MORE · BINGO

EARL-Y END FOR ESSEX

Robert, Earl of Essex, was always a hothead. Today he became a *no*-head when the executioner's axe had finished with him. His enemies would like to have seen him hanged and gutted like the traitor he was, but the Queen spared her one-time favourite.

The Queen called the Earl her 'Wild Horse', and spent years putting up with Essex (34) and his moods.

He could be charming when he wanted and the handsome young tearaway knew how to flatter the old Queen.

The Earl thought the people of England were ready for a new leader. There have been years of famine in which poor people have died on the streets or fed their children on cats, dogs and nettle roots. Essex decided he was the man to lead them into a new century and a new age. He rode at the head of 100 horsemen into the city of London. But the 'most popular man in England' (as he has been called) found that no one would join him.

He was arrested and the Queen's only mercy was to let him be beheaded. Today is a sad day for Her Majesty. Her people still support her but the last of her young favourites is dead. She'll be lonely now with nothing to look forward to but death.

Liz's loo

Queen Elizabeth travelled around the south of England and stayed in the houses of gentlemen and ladies. If you ever got a letter from the Queen saying, 'I am coming to stay with you!' then you might have been thrilled.

You might also have been horrified. The Queen's careless courtiers could easily leave your home a wreck.

Queen Liz expected…

- your best rooms for herself and her lords (while you moved out and lived in an inn or a tent).
- rich gifts – gold and jewels were best.
- entertainments – music, plays and sports.

216

The honour was great … but the cost could be greater. It wasn't just the homes of gentlemen that had to fork out. It was the ordinary people of the places she visited.

A grammar school in Norwich paid out nine shillings and four pence (two weeks' wages for a teacher) just to paint the door and clean up three loads of 'street muck' outside. The nervous headmaster gave a speech (in Latin) and she let him kiss her hand. What a treat for Liz – would you like to have your hand kissed by a head-teacher?

Everywhere Elizabeth went, her people spent a fortune cleaning the place up. She must have thought England was a really tidy place!

On that visit to Norwich the people of the city were given orders weeks before she arrived…

Put fresh plaster on the fronts of your houses (just the side the queen would see)

• Clean up your outside toilets

• Repair the path outside your house

• Keep your cows off the streets – milk them in the fields or your yard

• Sweep your chimneys (fine for a chimney fire – 6 shillings and 8 pence)

In addition, butchers who killed cattle inside the city had to take the waste outside and bury it. Makes you wonder what they did with it before. No cows, pigs or horses were to be kept in the castle ditch.

Why did Elizabeth make her people go to all this trouble? There were two good reasons … and one other that most history books don't mention...

1 Elizabeth wanted her people to see her – she loved being cheered by her faithful subjects.

2 The plague came to London most summers and it was safer to travel round in the fresher air of the countryside.[1]

3 Toilets.

Toilets? (You are probably asking yourself!) What have *toilets* got to do with the Queen going on a tour about the countryside. (Even if you are *not* asking yourself this, you are going to be told.)

In Tudor England the great houses and palaces had little rooms just like in your house. The Tudor name was 'jakes'. But the waste from the jakes didn't get washed away. It fell

1. But the court often brought the plague with it and hundreds of townspeople died after Elizabeth left. After the Queen left Norwich, 5,000 people died of plague. Some of her hosts were dead honoured after her visit – others were simply dead.

down into a pit. With hundreds of people living in a palace these pits soon filled up … and up … and up.

The pits had to be opened up, the waste shovelled up and carted away. (There's a nice job for someone … preferably someone without a sense of smell.)

While this was going on it was pretty disgusting in your palace. The smell would hang around for weeks. The best thing to do would be to fill up your jakes, then move out while they were emptied. That's what the Tudor monarchs did. That's why they had three or four palaces and kept moving around. Best of all, Elizabeth could move around to other people's houses and fill up *their* jakes! Then she could move on and leave some other poor person (or poo person) to clear up after her.

What is the greatest gift you could give your queen? A pair of golden spurs? A pair of jewelled gloves? A pair of solid silver nose-hair clippers?

No. It would be a flushing toilet. And that's just what her godson, Sir John Harrington did…

21 May 1589

Your most Illustrious and beautiful majesty,

It is almost six years now since you banished me from court. I deserved it. The joke I made about Kate Sedley's chest was extremely rude and I quite understand why she was so upset. I also understand why you told me to leave your palace and never return.

But you are my Godmother and such a sweet, kindly person, I thought perhaps you may have forgiven me enough to come and visit me. Let me tell you what I have been doing in the six years that I have been away.

Of course I was heart-broken at your displeasure. A day without seeing you is like a day without sunshine. I came home to my old family estate in Somerset and wept for weeks. Then I decided on my great project. I decided to build a new house, a great house, and a house with an invention so magical you would have to come and visit me.

You see, when I built Kelston Hall I built in a special toilet system. It works with water. The person entering the jakes sits on a comfortable wooden seat. When they have finished then they pull a lever and water from a tank above the toilet rushes down. The foul-smelling waste is washed away down drains to a deep pit. The result is the sweetest smelling house you ever imagined.

If you will excuse my little joke, I call my invention "Ajax" after the Greek hero – and because I invented "a jakes" Ha! You always did like my jokes, dear Godmother. But please, please come to Kelston Hall. Please forgive me and please inspect Ajax.

Your loving Godson

John

Suppose *you* were Queen Elizabeth. What would you do if you got a letter saying, 'I'm sorry about my rude joke six years ago but, if you forgive me, you could come and see my new toilet'?

What did Elizabeth do?

a) Ignore the letter.

b) Visit John and forgive him.

c) Have him drowned in his own toilet bowl.

Answer:

b) The Queen was in a forgiving mood. She went across to Kelston Hall in the summer of 1591 and used the Ajax. She was delighted with it! Not only did she forgive her godson, but she invited him back to London to fit his toilet invention in all of her palaces.

Elizabeth was the first monarch in Britain to have a flushing toilet. It was healthier – and far less smelly – than the old jakes, yet it was another 200 years before the idea really caught on and was used in a lot of houses.

Quick quiz
What did the Elizabethans use instead of toilet paper?

Answer:

A damp rag. It could be rinsed and used over again. (Oh, stop pulling a disgusted face. It was probably better than the hard toilet paper your mum and dad used to use!)

In really nasty prisons you weren't even given a cloth. And you thought school detention was bad?

Would you believe it?

Here are some curious tales about the days of Queen Liz. But which are true and which are false? Pester your parent and blow their brain cell with this quick quiz.

1 Queen Elizabeth ate a chessboard.

2 In her last years Elizabeth carried a rusty old sword around her palace in case she was attacked.

3 Elizabeth stayed alive with the help of expensive medicines.

4 John Stubbs wrote and criticized Elizabeth's plan to marry a Frenchman, so Elizabeth had Stubbs's hand cut off.

5 When the Spanish Armada sailed to England, Elizabeth was brave and ready to face them.

6 When sister Mary Tudor was queen, Elizabeth wore finer dresses than Mary.

7 Elizabeth invented the nickname 'Bloody Mary' for her sister.

8 When Queen Mary died she left a will. Elizabeth ignored it.

9 Elizabeth's pet name for Sir Walter Raleigh was 'Water'.

10 Elizabeth kept her breath fresh with mint mouthwash.

Answers:

1 True. It was made from her favourite food – marzipan – shaped into black and white squares. In fact she ate so much of this sticky sweet that it rotted her teeth till they were as black and white as the chessboard ... mate!

2 True. She was terrified of being assassinated. A sailor and a gang of men burst into the room where she was eating with her ladies-in-waiting. He had already drawn his dagger to strike before the guards managed to stop him. Elizabeth banned her courtiers from wearing long cloaks because she wanted their swords uncovered and ready – she even threatened to pass a law against long cloaks! (And Little Red Riding Hood would have had to change her name to Little Red Bomber Jacket!)

3 False. Elizabeth hated taking medicine. She kept fit with lots of walking and riding. The doctors said all the exercise  would kill her but in fact in the last six years of her reign she had five different doctors ... and they all died before her! In the end she went for walkies in the rain, caught a cold and never recovered. If the Queen had had a pair of wellies she might have lived even longer.

4 True. Elizabeth considered marrying Francis, Duke of Anjou but many English people were horrified because he was a Catholic. Stubbs was brave enough (or stupid enough) to write a leaflet attacking her. The punishment was to cut off the hand that wrote it. Stubbs used his remaining hand to wave his hat in the air and cry, 'God save the Queen!' ...

before he fainted. The publisher also had his hand cut off – a sharp lesson to all publishers who write nasty things about the royal family!

5 False (probably). She is famous for her speech to the troops as they waited for the Spanish to land: 'I have the body of a weak and feeble woman, but I have the heart and stomach of a king.' Modern historians are not sure if she really made the speech … but, even if she did, not many would have heard it. As for her courage, a lot of her soldiers said she had none.

6 False. Elizabeth was crafty. Her supporters were the Protestants who hated flashy clothes. Elizabeth wore black and white to please them. Mary was angry and wanted Elizabeth to dress in rich materials with jewels. Once Mary died and Elizabeth became queen, *then* she gave up the plain clothes and wore dresses encrusted with jewels. The dresses could stand up by themselves!

7 False. Mary I is usually known as Bloody Mary but no one in Tudor times called her that. They probably wouldn't dare! The name was invented about a hundred years after her death. In Mary's own time she was called 'a raging madwoman' and 'mischievous Mary'.

8 True. Elizabeth didn't become a Catholic as Mary had asked, she didn't bury Catherine of Aragon beside her daughter Mary and she certainly didn't give King Philip of Spain his jewels back!

9 True. But it wasn't because he was wet. Sir Walter came from Devon and spoke with a strong Devon accent. When he said, 'My name is Walter,' it sounded like, 'My name is Water.' Water funny thing to say!

10 False. Elizabeth used a mixture with lots of sugar in it. Of course, this rotted her teeth. Good dentists said Tudor people should use wooden toothpicks and they were right. But rich people used gold or silver ones that damaged their teeth. So, if you want to suffer like Liz then rinse your mouth out with lemonade three times a day and the tooth fairy will be a regular visitor to your house!

Devilish Doctor Dee
John Dee (1527–1608)

In Tudor England witches were tortured and hanged. But if you were queen of England you could use witchcraft and get away with it. Elizabeth I had her own pet witch – a mathematician called John Dee. And in Elizabethan times many people thought mathematics was an art practised by witches!

Try telling that to your maths teacher…

In 1534, a nun was hanged because she foretold the future – she said Henry VIII would die within a month if he married Anne Boleyn. But Queen Elizabeth invited Doctor Dee to read her horoscope, foretell the future and pick the best date for her coronation. He wasn't hanged, he was rewarded.

One law for Liz, another for the poor!

In 1569 a new law said it was a crime to speak with evil spirits. But Doctor Dee chatted away with a spirit girl called Madini and was never punished. Why not? Because he was a friend of the Queen.

One law for Liz, another for the poor!

The law may not have punished Doctor Dee but the people near his London home did. His home was raided while he was away. His science equipment was destroyed and his valuable collection of books was ruined. That sounds like a useful story...

Of course Elizabeth didn't just use witchcraft – she was a *target* of witchcraft too. In 1577 a wax model of the Queen was found in London with a pin stuck through the heart – this was a trick that witches use to harm an enemy. John Dee was called in to stop the magic working on Elizabeth.

John Dee was clever. But his partner, Edward Kelly, was crafty. For years Edward Kelly tricked John Dee. The one who suffered more than any was Dee's second wife, Joan. If she could have told her story it may have been something like this...

The Magic of Madini

Edward Kelley is dead. Today we heard the news. Kelley had been working in Prague for the Emperor and getting well paid. Paid to produce gold from lead, of course. That old trick. The philosopher's stone, they call it. Anyway, the Emperor became impatient when Kelley failed to produce the gold and had him locked away. As Kelley climbed a wall to escape, he slipped and fell. He broke both his legs and his injuries killed him.

It's hard to feel sorry for him after the years of misery he put me through. Kelley was a sneaky, evil man who looked like a devil with his black skull cap pulled tightly down over his head. The cap never bulged where his ears should be and that's what made me first suspect him.

'He was a wonderful man,' my husband, Master Dee, said.

He still believed it! Now I'm not one to destroy a man's dreams but there comes a time when it is kinder to. So I said, 'He was a fake and a fraud and a trickster.'

John blinked. 'Oh, Joan, no! I saw him myself. Speaking to angels! No other living person had his skill!'

'Exactly!' I said. 'That's all it was. A skill. He *pretended* to speak to angels and you believed him because you wanted to.'

John turned pale and sat down suddenly.

He picked up the crystal ball that always sat on his desk – his 'show stone', he called it. 'Edward Kelley saw visions in here. He spoke to them.'

'He said he heard them. But you never did.'

John waved a bony finger at me. 'But I heard them rapping when I asked them questions. Edward Kelley couldn't have been doing the rapping,' he said. 'Our hands were joined on the tabletop. They never moved.'

'Ah, but I went into the room after you'd finished. It was the smell of stinking feet. That's what gave him away.'

'Did it? How?'

'Think about it, John. I did.'

He frowned. 'But Edward Kelley made gold from iron. He cut a piece from the bottom of a frying pan. He heated it in a crucible with his philosopher's stone, stirred it with his metal rod and poured out liquid gold. You saw the gold yourself before we sent it to the Queen.'

'I also saw the stirring rod he left behind,' I said.

'What about it?'

'It wasn't a solid rod. It was a metal tube.'

'So?'

I sighed. 'John, you *want* to believe Edward Kelley helped you speak to angels. The local people think it was devils you spoke to. That's why they hate us. You *want* to believe that Kelley made gold. The Emperor in Prague didn't believe him and that's why he locked him away. You want to believe Kelley was an honest man, but I know why he wore that skull cap.'

John Dee is clever, but it took him a few days to think over what I'd said. It was a week later that he came to me and said, 'I've been a fool, Joan.'

We sat down and, together, we talked of how Edward Kelley had fooled John Dee – the cleverest fool in Elizabeth's England!

Can you work it out? How did Joan know that Kelley was a fake? What was the importance of the skull cap? The scent of dirty feet? And the stirring tube?

Answers:

1 The skull cap Edward Kelley had been a villain all his life. He was charged with forgery at Lancaster. His punishment was to have his head placed in a pillory and his ears nailed to the wood. His ears were then cropped off

PIERCED EARS

and left nailed to the pillory as a warning to others. Everyone in Tudor England would know that a man without ears was a cheat and a liar. So Kelley wore the black cap to hide the fact.

It is said that Doctor John Dee knew Kelley for almost ten years and *never* discovered that his ears had been cut off!

2 The rapping In Victorian times there were groups of people who believed they could contact the dead. They called themselves 'spiritualists' and they spoke to the dead through a 'medium'. While they held hands with the medium there were rapping sounds on the table or floor, just as there were when Kelley performed with the 'show stone'. But investigators discovered that a good medium trained his or her toes to be as nimble as fingers. They held rods with their feet and could rap on wood to create the effect of talking to a spirit. It's likely that Kelley used this sort of trick – but would be betrayed by smelly feet!

3 The philosopher's stone Kelley said he found two powders (one red and one white) in Glastonbury where the mystical King Arthur is supposed to be buried. He succeeded in making iron into gold. But, of course, it was a trick. Here's how to do it...

1 First, prepare your stirring rod. Take a hollow tube, pack in 50 g of gold dust and plug the end with candle wax.

2 While your audience is watching, cut a piece of iron from a pan. Make sure the iron piece is less than 50 g in weight.

3 Heat a crucible over a flame. Pretend to drop the iron piece into the crucible but slip it into your pocket.

4 Sprinkle a little red powder and a little white powder into the crucible. Then take the stirring rod and stir the powder.

5 The wax plug will melt, and the gold dust will fall into the crucible and melt.

6 Place the iron pan on a cold surface (like a tile). Pour the gold into the cut-out hole and let it cool. You will have a piece of gold the shape of the cut-out.

7 Sell the powder (which can be chalk dust) to the audience. Sell it for a great deal of money.

8 Have a very fast horse waiting and ride off as fast as you can before they discover the philosopher's stone is worthless and you deserve to hang!

233

Another trick was to boil lead and gold in a crucible. The lead boiled away and left pure gold. It looked as if you had turned the lead into gold. It cost you a little money to buy the gold in the first place, but you could make a fortune if you worked the trick well.

John Dee tried and tried to make gold from ordinary metal after Kelley left the country. He was puzzled because it failed! Dee was lucky because the Queen liked him and forgave him. Elizabeth saw another magician who failed and had him thrown into the Tower of London!

But John Dee did come up with one good idea that made Elizabeth a fortune. One of his maths skills was in map-making. It is probable that he showed the Queen how it would be possible for English ships to reach South America and return safely.

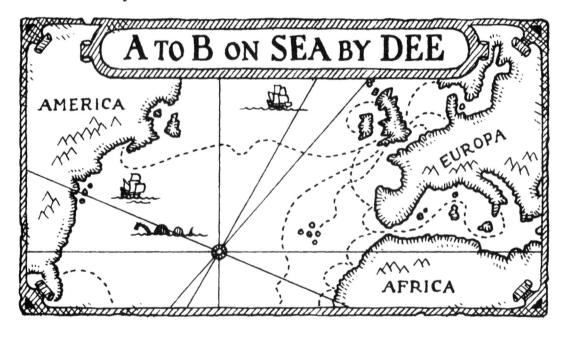

All the Queen needed was a skilful sailor who could follow Dee's charts and be bold enough to attack every Spanish port and Spanish ship he found there. There was one man who was just right for the job – a brilliant sailor and a ruthless pirate – Francis Drake.

Drake the quacker
Sir Francis Drake (1542–1596)

When it came to making money, Queen Elizabeth was ruthless. She looked greedily at the Spanish treasure ships and decided she wanted her share.

The Spanish didn't like Elizabeth and her England too much. After all, the Spanish king, Philip, had been married to her sister, Mary…

And, of course, Elizabeth was a protestant…

So, the Spanish didn't like the English. They weren't going to give Queen Liz their silver…

Elizabeth told Drake she would 'gladly be revenged on the King of Spain' … but the money was as important as the revenge.

It took a lot of setting up. Someone had to pay for Drake's

ships, pay for the supplies and a crew. Would you risk your money on Captain Drake? If the adventure went well you'd get a share of the treasure. But it was a risk. If storms or Spanish galleons sank Drake's ships then you'd lose all of your money.

There is one way you could keep a check on how your money is being spent. Go along on the voyage with Drake! What a great idea!

Francis's fury

Thomas Doughty thought it was a good idea to put money into the trip and sail along with Drake. In fact, it was the worst idea of his life. Doughty was a gentleman and very proud of it.

Drake was a poor, common man – but just as proud as Doughty. Drake was in charge of the expedition and gave the orders. Doughty hated taking orders from this common seaman.

The trouble began when Drake captured a Portuguese ship...

NO ONE TOUCHES THE PRISONERS OR THEIR TREASURE

But Doughty took a gift from the Portuguese prisoners. Gloves, coins and a ring. When Drake saw them he was furious...

DOUGHTY, YOU ARE UNDER ARREST

Gentleman Doughty was sent to one of the smaller ships where he was half-starved and told to eat the toilet waste that fell over the anchor chain. He plotted his revenge and told the crew of his ship…

When Drake got to hear of this he called all his crew ashore for a trial…

The trial went ahead and Doughty was found guilty. Drake then offered Doughty a choice...

HOW WOULD YOU LIKE TO DIE? I CAN PUT A BULLET THROUGH YOUR HEAD MYSELF

GENTLEMEN ARE BEHEADED!

Drake gave Doughty two days to make his will and say his prayers. Then they had dinner together and chatted in a friendly way before the execution. Doughty spoke to the crew and wished them luck before he placed his head on the block.

His head was struck off and Drake raised it in the air...

This is the end of all traitors.

Drake added that this would be the end of anyone else who wanted to argue with him. No one did!

He went on to loot a fortune in Spanish treasure and returned to England by sailing all the way around the world.

When Drake got back to England, three years later, Doughty's family tried to have him charged with murdering Thomas. Elizabeth said that Drake could only be arrested by the Constable of England ... but, sadly, England didn't have a Constable at that time, so Drake would have to go free!

Why was Elizabeth so kind to Drake? Could it be something to do with the fortune in silver, jewels, spices and cloth he returned with?.

For every £1 the Queen paid towards the trip she got £47 in return! Everyone who put money into the adventure became very rich … except Thomas Doughty, of course, who became very dead.

Francis's fun

Francis Drake was not usually seen as a cruel man – even by his deadly Spanish enemies. But one trick was a bit vicious.

Drake's men captured a Spanish ship in a South American harbour. Most of the crew had jumped overboard and swam ashore, but Drake captured one young sailor alive. There was no treasure loaded on to the ship. It must be somewhere on shore. Drake didn't want to waste time looking for it.

He turned to his captive. 'Tell me where I'll find the silver when I get ashore.'

'I'll tell you nothing,' the brave young Spaniard said.

'Tell me or I'll hang you.'

'You are not a murderer, Captain Drake. You won't hang me.'

'Won't I?' Drake laughed. He ordered a rope to be thrown over one of the ship's spars. He tied the sailor's hands and stood him on the edge of the ship. Then he placed the rope around his neck. 'Now will you tell me?'

The Spaniard trembled, shook his head and said, 'You wouldn't.'

239

'Wouldn't I?' Drake placed a hand against the young man's knee and pushed him till he tumbled off the side of the ship.

The sailor screamed as he fell and the scream stopped only when the sailor hit the water. The rope around his neck had not been fastened to anything and it didn't choke the prisoner. Drake told him to hold on to the rope and hauled him back on the ship. By now the man was so terrified he told Drake everything he wanted to know.

That's cruel.

Francis's failure

In 1580 Francis Drake was knighted by the Queen for his efforts. He was her favourite feller. Of course the Queen said, 'Let's do it again!'

In 1585 she paid half of the £40,000 costs to send Drake back to South America. Of course, the Spanish were ready for him this time and he was beaten again and again. He returned with just £30,000 in treasure – the Queen lost £5,000 and Drake lost 750 men, including some of his best captains.

Queen Elizabeth was Misery Liz. Drake wasn't her pet any longer.

But Spain's king was Furious Phil. He sent the great Armada, a fleet of 130 ships, against England in 1588 and

Drake helped to defeat it. Drake was back in favour.

The Queen decided to follow the Spanish back to their home and destroy their ships before they could send another armada against England. In 1589 Drake was put in charge of the attack on Spain … and failed. No treasure and over 10,000 men dead this time! Misery Liz again!

So Drake offered to go on one more voyage to the Americas to steal Spanish treasure in 1595. He was sick and old now and it wasn't a Spanish cannon that finished him off. It was much sadder.

Many poems have been written about Drake, the great hero. A lot of the poems were written by his old enemies, the Spanish.

In one poem, he is poisoned by his English sailors because he failed on his last expedition. This spiteful Spanish verse ended…

'I come, I come; oh fearful Death, I come!'
With that Drake died, his frozen tongue was still.
The staring pupils flickered now no more;
The purple mouth, cold with the chill of death,
Spat out his wicked soul; out from his breast
Into the deep and endless mouth of Hell.

Cheerful stuff, but nonsense. Here is the horrible historical truth...

Dead duck Drake

Drake was in the Indies and he wasn't doing well.
His men were falling sick, and dropping dead.
The Spanish sailors fought real hard, and gave the
* English hell.*
'Ohhhh! I don't feel too grand,' Sir Francis said.

He lay down in his cabin and the fever made him sick.
The doctor said, 'You'll die before you're older!'
Then Drake he made his will and he said, 'Bring my
* armour quick!*
If I'm to die then I'll die like a soldier!'
He fastened on his armour then he lay down on his bed,
His sailors gathered round to say goodbye.
Within an hour the brave old Francis Drake was lying
* dead,*
And tears ran down from every sailor's eye.

They wrapped his poor old body in a coffin made of lead,
So fishes couldn't eat him and get fat.
They dropped the coffin in the sea. 'Goodbye old Drake,'
* they said.*
They sailed back home again ... and that was that!

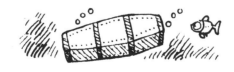

Mary Queen of chops

Mary Queen of Scots: Queen in Scotland (reigned 1542–1568) Died 1587.

Mary Queen of Scots became queen of Scotland when she was just six days old. (She probably celebrated by wetting her nappy.) Her great grandfather was Henry VII, so she was a Tudor. That meant she enjoyed plotting and murdering her enemies, not to mention her friends and relatives. Being a Tudor, she got away with it – until she came up against *another* Tudor, that is!

Mary was forced to leave Scotland when she got into a bit of trouble for having her husband murdered. (He deserved it.) She fled to England and asked for cousin Elizabeth's protection. Elizabeth I had Mary arrested and locked away for 19 years. But there were always Catholics plotting to kill Elizabeth and put Mary on the throne of England. Mary had to go.

Elizabeth always said she didn't want the blame for killing cousin Mary, but...

- Elizabeth's spies trapped Mary into saying she wanted Elizabeth dead, then...
- After a trial, Elizabeth signed Mary's death warrant, though...
- Elizabeth sent a message to Mary's jailer suggesting it would be better if Mary was quietly murdered!

When the jailer refused to murder Mary Queen of Scots then the execution had to go ahead. These are the foul facts...

Foul facts about Mary's execution

1 Mary didn't know she was going to die till the night before it happened. She stayed awake all night, writing letters and praying. It would have been difficult to sleep, anyway, with guards marching up and down outside her room and the scaffold being hammered together in the great hall. By the time she got to the block she must have been ready to nod off!

2 Mary's jailers refused to let her have a Catholic priest to pray with her. This was a bit spiteful. They gave her a Protestant who was still trying to convert her when she was on the scaffold! She simply said, 'I've lived a Catholic, so I will die a Catholic.' This didn't stop him going on and on.

3 Mary's servants read a Bible story with her. It was the story of the good thief who died on the cross alongside Jesus. Mary heard it and said, 'That thief was a great sinner – but not such a great sinner as I have been.' Maybe she was thinking of the husband she had murdered.

4 The Scottish Queen was not allowed to die quietly. Three hundred people crowded into the hall to watch her execution. The scaffold was decorated in a delightful shade of black and it made a very pleasant day out for the spectators. Some reported that she came into the hall 'cheerful and smiling', so that was all right.

5 Mary was dressed in black until the time came for her to die. She took her dress off and was wearing a red petticoat. She slipped on red sleeves and was all in red, so the blood wouldn't show. That's tidy, isn't it? She wore a turban round her head to keep her hair out of the way of the axe. Her eyes were bound with a white cloth, trimmed in gold.

6 The axe-man's assistant held her body steady while the axe fell. It missed the neck and cut into the back of her head. Her servants later said they heard her mutter, 'Sweet Jesus.' The second chop was a better shot but it still needed a bit of sawing with the axe to finish it off.

7 Mary's pet dog, a skye terrier, had slipped into the hall under the cover of her skirts and was still hiding there when her head was lopped off. It finally came out, whimpering. It's said that the dog refused to eat and pined away and died.

8 Mary's heart was removed – the English didn't want any of that Robert the Bruce nonsense with loyal Scots following a heart into battle. The heart was buried in the castle grounds and hasn't been seen since. Mary asked to be buried in France. So, of course, she was buried in Peterborough, which is not the same thing at all. In 1612, her son, by then James I of England, had her coffin moved to Westminster Abbey where it is today.

Meanwhile, at Fotheringhay, the Scottish national flower, the thistle, was growing. People said they sprang from the tears of Mary Queen of Scots.

Gloriana the gory

The Elizabethan age is famous for its theatre. Great writers like Shakespeare and Marlowe began to create plays which are performed all around the world to this day. One of the greatest fans was the Queen herself (nicknamed Gloriana).

But where did these great plays come from? Did William Shakespeare just sit down one day and say...

Of course not. In the Middle Ages, the workers in the towns had produced religious plays, often based on Bible stories. But they weren't just a way of preaching to people on stage. They were FUN...

Devils sprang from trapdoors. God and his angels swooped down from cranes. Hell's mouth opened and belched out smoke. Floods, fires and earthquakes were staged. Characters suffered gory executions and wounds. Animals like rabbits and rams appeared as sacrifices. Costumes and masks were dazzling. Singing and dancing was loud and lively.

Henry VIII's chopping and changing of the Church changed all that.

What a loss! Imagine if today's Queen pulled the plug on all your television! People would miss it.

Poets started writing plays for students to perform in their colleges. A teacher, Nicholas Udal, wrote a play for his pupils to perform in front of Elizabeth.

But what could the ordinary people do for fun?

There were street entertainers doing disgusting things for money. One man pretended to stab himself in the stomach. In

fact, he had a bag of pig's blood under his shirt and a wooden shield under that. When he was stabbed, the pig's blood spurted out and the audience gasped with wonder (or threw up in horror). One drunken entertainer forgot the shield one day, stabbed himself in the stomach and died. The audience thought that was the best trick they'd ever seen!

A juggler called Kingsfield showed the body of 'John the Baptist' who'd had his head cut off – the head lay at the feet and it spoke!

Then there was always the torturing of animals for sport.

In the courtyards of inns and special buildings there was cock-fighting, bear-baiting and bull-baiting. In 1584 a foreign visitor to the Beargarden in London described the cheerful little scene…

> *There is a round building three stories high in which are kept about a hundred large English dogs, with separate wooden kennels for each of them. These dogs were made to fight one at a time with three bears, the second bear being larger than the first and the third larger than the second. After this a horse was brought in and chased by the dogs and, at the end, a bull who defended himself bravely.*

The trouble is the bears needed a rest every other day. What could the bear-pit owners do to entertain the Elizabethans on the bear's day off? Put on the plays!

Don't give them the clever poetic plays of the students. Give them a bit of the old glamour and guts of the old religious plays.

But don't give them the religion of those old plays, of course – religion could get you hanged, burned and chopped in Tudor times!

Instead they went back to the Roman theatre. They took

ideas from writers like Seneca. His favourite subjects were crime and revenge, witches and ghosts, and they were very popular. The Romans loved tales of horror. Shakespeare probably read Seneca's gruesome plays at school.

William Shakespeare was a clever man. When he started writing at the end of the 1580s he was going to give the Beargarden mob the sort of fun they wanted ... he was going to give them *horror*.

If the plays of the Elizabethan playwrights Marlowe, Kyd and Shakespeare were produced today they would be given an '18' certificate.

Terrible Titus

Titus Andronicus was probably one of Shakespeare's earliest plays. You won't see it performed much these days. Here's this charming tale of family fun ... and fingernails.

Perform this potted play for school governors, parents and teachers. But have the sick-bags handy.

Cast:

Titus Andronicus – old Roman general, losing his marbles.

Lucius – Titus's last-remaining son.

Tamora – Queen of the defeated Goths, prisoner of Titus and a nasty piece of work.

Alarbus – eldest son of Tamora and quite inflammable.

Chiron and Demetrius – Tamora's younger sons. Suckers.

Aaron – Tamora's boyfriend. A bit of a stirrer and a lot of a murderer.

Bassianus and Saturninus – Sons of the dead Roman emperor. Not very brotherly.

Lavinia – Titus's daughter. Engaged to Saturninus till Bassianus snatches her and she is really cut up about it.

Servants can be played by those who die early on in the play.

Scene 1 – Titus's palace in Rome.
(Titus and Tamora meet)

Titus: Oh dear! Oh dear! Oh dear! Twenty-five sons I had at one time! Twenty-five! And how many have I got now? Four! After that battle with *your* Goths! Four! It's all your fault, Tamora. I'm going to have your oldest lad executed.

Tamora: You can't do that, you swine! That's not fair!

Titus: Bassianus and Saturninus! Fetch Tamora's son.

(Enter Bassianus and Saturninus with Alarbus)

Bassianus: Yes, General.

Titus: Take Tamora's son, Alarbus. Take him to the altar, cut him into pieces then burn him as a sacrifice to my dead sons.

Alarbus: That's not very fair, Mum!

Tamora: I told him that, son, but the old fool won't listen.

Alarbus: *(Led off by Bassianus)* Bye, Mum.

Tamora: Bye, son.

Titus: As for *you*, Saturninus … I do not want the job of emperor. I hereby elect you!

Saturninus: Thanks, boss!

Titus: And you can marry my daughter, Lavinia.

Saturninus: Even better. This is my lucky day!

Alarbus: *(Voice from off-stage)* I wish it was mine! Ouch!

(They all leave the stage. Enter Lucius.)

Lucius: *(Narrating)* Before Lavinia could marry Saturninus, she saw Tamora's boyfriend, Aaron, kill Bassianus. To silence her Aaron cut out her tongue. To stop her writing the name of the killer he cut off her hands. Titus saw one of his sons killed by Bassianus and another two murdered by Saturninus – even though Titus had cut off his own hand in an attempt to get mercy for them. That left me, Lucius, as his last son and handless Lavinia as his last daughter.

Titus: So who did this to you, Lavinia? Here … take this stick and write it in the sand … *(He reads)* Tamora! Fetch her sons, Chiron and Demetrius to me Lavinia … and fetch a big bowl.

(Lavinia enters with Chiron and Demetrius)

Chiron: What can I do for you, old chap?

Titus: Kneel down, boys. Now, Lavinia, hold that bowl to catch the blood while I cut their throats. *(Chiron and Demetrius try to run. Titus catches them off-stage. Lavinia hurries after with the bowl.)*

Scene 2 – The palace a few days later.
(Enter Tamora and Saturninus, Titus, Lavinia and Lucius)

Titus: Have this nice pie I had specially baked.

Tamora: *(Helping herself)* Yummy! But hang on – yeuch! This is a human fingernail!

Titus: That's right. You have ruined my daughter's life. There's nothing left for her but death. So, here it is! *(He stabs Lavinia)*

Tamora: Never mind her! What was in that pie?

Titus: Your last two sons … Chiron and Demetrius. You've just eaten them!

Tamora: Yeuuuurrrrggggh!

Titus: Now it's your turn, Queen terrible Tamora! *(He stabs Tamora)*

Saturninus: Now it's your turn, old twithead Titus! *(He stabs Titus)*

Lucius: Now it's your turn, savage Saturninus! *(He stabs Saturninus then calls …)* Servants! Feed Tamora to the wild beasts and bury the rest. *(To audience)* I guess that makes me emperor since I'm the last one left alive! The end!

That was Elizabeth's entertainment. Murders, executions and sacrifices – heads and hands cut off, on stage. Sons served up in a pie to their mother.

Queen Elizabeth loved it – and so would you, probably. But would your parents let you watch it?

Compared to the real-life, bloodthirsty executions, of course, the blood on the stage was just harmless fun!

No Kydding

In *Titus Andronicus*, Shakespeare was trying to grab the attention of his horror-loving audience. But he was still putting plenty of gore and shocks into his plays ten or 20 years later. Shakespeare shockers included…

• a character having his eyes ripped out on stage *(King Lear)*

• a king beheaded in a sword fight *(Macbeth)*

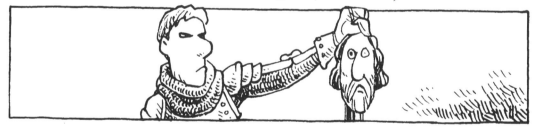

• a real bear chasing a character off the stage *(The Winter's Tale)*.

But at least Shakespeare lived a fairly peaceful life himself, unlike some of his fellow playwrights.

Thomas Kyd wrote *The Spanish Tragedy* – probably before Shakespeare's terrifying *Titus Andronicus*. It was a huge success and was still being performed 50 years after it was written. He died after being tortured as a Catholic spy at the age of 36.

Marlowe died in a mysterious stabbing in 1593 aged just 29.

Why was Shakespeare the greatest Elizabethan playwright? Because he survived longer than his rivals!

Test your Tudor teacher

Teachers don't know everything. Amazing but true! But they test you and expect you to know it. So it's only fair they should face a sort of Tudor torture. (Or the threat of double helpings of school dinner should have them begging for mercy!)

1 The Spanish had a nickname for Francis Drake, 'El Draco'. Draco sounds like Drake, but what does 'El Draco' mean?

a) The dragon.
b) The pirate.
c) Red-beard.

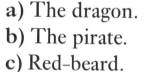

2 Queen Elizabeth gave nicknames to all her close friends. Some were kind but some were cruel. What did she call the French Duke of Anjou who proposed marriage to her?

a) Ou la la.
b) Big Al.
c) Frog.

3 Henry VIII wanted to make an example of the religious rebels in 1537. He had them hanged in a special place. Where?

a) In the Tower of London so the whole city could see them.

b) In their gardens so their wives and children could see them.

c) From the masts of ships so they could tour the country and be seen in every port.

4 Anne Boleyn rode through London on her way to be crowned queen. Few people cheered and some even booed the unpopular queen. But what did the teenage apprentice lads do?

a) Whistled at Anne as she rode past.

b) Laughed, 'HA! HA!'

c) Sang, *God Save the Queen!*

5 One of Elizabeth's courtiers wore a new jerkin with tassels. She said, cruelly, 'Your mind is like your jerkin – gone to rags.' The poor man tried to explain they weren't ragged edges but tassels. What did Queen Liz do next?

a) Cut his tassels off with a knife.

b) Had a copy made for herself.

c) Spat on his new jerkin.

6 Henry VII sent the Earl of Warwick to the scaffold for plotting against him. In fact the Earl was not too bright. What did the Earl do on the short walk from his prison to the scaffold?

a) Got lost.

b) Tried to run away.

c) Snatched a guard's dagger and stabbed himself to death.

7 Henry VIII died on the morning of 28 January 1547. For the next three days what curious thing happened?

a) One by one his faithful dogs died of broken hearts.

b) Henry had all his meals served as usual.

c) The money that he kept in his room disappeared mysteriously.

8 In 1553, Lady Jane Grey was walking through a building that had once been a monastery (until Henry VIII closed it). Suddenly a bloodstained hand shot out through a gap in the wall waving an axe dripping with blood. What was it?

a) The ghost of a murdered monk who wanted revenge on the Tudor Lady.

b) Lady Jane had walked in on a cookery class for the monks.

c) A mad monk wanted to scare the Tudor away.

9 Lady Jane Grey's father, the Earl of Suffolk, was beheaded. What happened to his head?

a) It was preserved and put on display for 400 years.

b) Suffolk was pardoned so the head was sewn back on and he was buried.

c) It was stuck on a pike and displayed over London Bridge.

10 Henry VIII was famous as a great sportsman. But one sporting activity nearly killed him. Was it...?

a) A long jump.

b) A pole vault.

c) A javelin.

Answers:

1a) 'El Draco' means 'the dragon' and Drake was a monster to the Spanish. Of course he did not have scales, wings or claws and he only breathed fire when he set his beard on fire in mistake for his pipe.

2c) She called the Frenchman 'Frog' because the French, even then, were famous for eating frogs' legs.

ZISS IZ VRY STRARNGE, NO? ZEE ENGLISH EAT DRUMSTICKS, BUT DO WE CALL ZEM CHICKENS?

3b) That's pretty nasty isn't it? It's not enough that your poor old dad has been executed. But he's left swinging in your back garden so he gets in the way when you want a game of football with your friends.

4b) Special arches were placed over the road and decorated with crimson banners. Written in white letters were Henry and Anne's initials. H-A. The apprentice boys pointed at them and went 'HA! HA!' If Henry had any sense he'd have married someone called Isobel-Philippa ... and they'd have been cheered all the way!

5c) Her Majesty walked up to the man and spat on the new clothes. He was so ashamed he left the court and never returned. Her ladies-in-waiting were terrified that their dresses would be too fine. The jealous Queen hated that.

6a) The Earl of Warwick was said not to know 'a goose from a chicken'. He wandered out of his prison and headed in the wrong direction because he didn't seem to understand that the scaffold over there was for him. Two guards herded him back and the pathetic young man died. He was not clever enough to plot against Henry VII. But, as long as he lived, there would be supporters who might raise an army to set him free. Henry probably invented the 'plot' charge so Warwick's death was murder, really. Not unusual for a Tudor monarch.

7b) Henry's death meant the country was without a leader until young Edward's protector could sort things out. Enemies could have attacked while England was leaderless. So foreign visitors were told, 'King Henry VIII is a little poorly but he's still eating well.' Then Henry's meals were carried up to his room with an escort of blasting trumpets. Not even the loudest trumpets would wake the old corpse and it's for certain he didn't enjoy those meals! (But his hounds probably did.)

8c) An avenging monk wanted to scare the Tudor Lady away from the old building. A bloodstained axe would be enough to scare the spots off a giraffe, but Lady Jane Grey didn't run. The really strange thing is that just a few months later Lady Jane was beheaded with an axe, stained with the blood of her husband. Creepy, eh?

9a) His head fell into sawdust steeped in 'tannin' – that's the stuff that turns animal skins into leather. Suffolk's head was preserved like leather and was put on show until the 1940s. It was finally buried in London – about a mile away from his 400-year-dead body. That second grave must have been quite a small one, but the family still put up a headstone. (*Head* stone, geddit?)

10b) In 1525 Henry went out hunting with his hawks. He carried a pole with him and used it to vault across ditches in the countryside. He ran at one ditch, planted the pole in the bottom and vaulted across … when the pole snapped because he was so heavy. He landed head-first in the mud and was stuck so fast he began to choke. A footman grabbed the royal ankles and pulled him to safety. No one laughed – they wouldn't dare – and no one called him an old stick-in-the-mud!

Epilogue

The Tudors came in with a charge of knights and flashing swords at the Battle of Bosworth Field. It was the last such charge in the history of England.

They went out with another great charge but it was the charge of a single horseman.

Queen Elizabeth I took too long to die. She became feeble and lost all the Tudor energy that had driven England for over 100 years. The country was like a car running out of petrol, slowly coasting to a stop. No one cared. Even the servants in her last palace at Richmond left the place filthy and uncared for.

Then, on the night of 23 March 1603, the Queen's lady-in-waiting, Philadelphia Scrope, crossed to a palace window and opened it. She slipped a sapphire ring off her finger and passed it out to her brother, Sir Robert Carey. It was the signal he'd been waiting for. A signal that the last Tudor was dead.

Even though Philadelphia and Robert were the Queen's cousins they weren't going to hang around and weep for the dead woman. They were going to make their fortune by being part of the future. Robert jumped on to the first of a string of fast horses he had arranged along the road north. He galloped through the city, past the carts loaded with victims of the latest plague, and out of the city.

By evening he was in Doncaster. Just 60 hours after leaving London he clattered into Edinburgh. He was bloodied from a fall on the road through the Borders, but King James VI of Scotland welcomed him and heard the news he'd been waiting for. 'Elizabeth is dead. You are named as the next king.'

The days of Tudor terror were over as the slimy Stuarts took over. That's another story for another book. But history is always like that. No sooner has the old died than the new takes over. The old are remembered and preserved in history books.

Some of the 'old' are remembered fondly. Henry VIII is remembered as a strong ruler and Elizabeth has been called the Queen of a 'golden age'. The pain and the misery they caused are often forgotten. To see the past clearly you don't just need history – you need horrible history. Some of the 'old' are remembered fondly. Henry VIII is remembered as a strong ruler and Elizabeth has been called the Queen of a 'golden age'. The pain and the misery they caused are often forgotten. To see the past clearly you don't just need history – you need horrible history

TERRIFYING TUDORS

GRISLY QUIZ

Now find out if you're a
Terrifying Tudors expert!

Quick questions

This was the age when the Tudor family brought terror to Britain. Brit sailors discovered new worlds and new ways to kill themselves – like tobacco – while Tudor Tower torturers found new ways to make you suffer. Even queenly necks were on the block while Henry's fat bum was on the throne.

1 In 1502 King James IV of Scotland fell in love with Margaret Drummond, but she died suddenly. What curious thing happened to her sister at the same time? (Clue: double trouble)

2 Henry VIII came to the throne in 1509. Two people had to die so he could become king. Who? (Clue: father and son)

3 In the 1514 Battle of Flodden between England and Scotland, the Earl of Surrey was carried into battle. Why? (Clue: no zimmer frames)

4 Queen Catherine was in charge of England when her army beat the Scots at Flodden because Henry VIII was in France. The Scottish king was hacked down. What gruesome gift did Catherine send Henry to celebrate the win? (Clue: James would be chilly without it)

5 In 1528 the Protestant Scottish rebel Patrick Hamilton was executed. Why was the damp weather bad news for poor Pat? (Clue: smoking is bad for your health)

6 In 1532 a cook, Richard Rosse, poisoned 17 people with his soup. He should have been hanged but Henry VIII thought of a more suitable way to execute a killer cook. What? (Clue: one for the pot)

7 In 1534 a fortune teller, the Holy Maid of Kent, said that Henry VIII would 'die a villain's death' if he married Anne Boleyn. Henry made sure that the Maid died a villain's death. How? (Clue: knot good)

8 In 1535 Henry's friend Thomas More was beheaded for opposing the king. Thomas warned the executioner about his neck. He said, 'Be careful because it's...' What? (Clue: no giraffe)

9 In 1536 Catherine of Aragon died and she was buried in a plain grave. But in Victorian times a group of ladies clubbed together to buy her a marble gravestone. What did they have in common with the dead queen? (Clue: not called Aragon)

10 In 1536 Queen Anne Boleyn was beheaded but not a drop of blood was spilled on the block? Why not? (Clue: someone swipes Anne's head!)

11 On 4 January 1540 Henry VIII was due to marry wife no. 4, Anne of Cleves, but he put it off for two days. Why? (Clue: you might do this with homework!)

12 In 1541 Henry headed off to York to meet the Scottish king, James V. What did James do that made Henry furious? (Clue: stand up?)

13 In 1541 the old Countess of Pole went to the block simply

because her son was Henry's enemy. Her behaviour was unusual. How? (Clue: catch me if you can)

14 In 1542 Henry had wife no. 5, Catherine Howard, executed for having boyfriends while she was married to him. He also executed Lady Rochford, Cathy's housekeeper. For what? (Clue: Cupid?)

15 In 1545 Henry VIII went to watch his magnificent warship, the Mary Rose, set sail to sort out the French. What did Mary Rose do to surprise the king? (Clue: behaves in a fishy manner)

16 In September 1546 Henry VIII was very ill. His doctors knew he was dying but they didn't tell him. Why not? (Clue: look what happened to the Holy Maid of Kent)

17 Henry VIII had his dinner delivered to his sick room on 31 January 1547, as he had done for the past month. What was so odd about this delivery? (Clue: he had no appetite)

18 Henry was buried in his huge coffin. There is a gruesome story that Catholic daughter Mary had his corpse dug up. Then what? (Clue: the first of many)

19 Edward VI came to the throne in 1547. Ed's pet dog warned him of a mysterious night-time visitor. What happened to the hero mutt? (Clue: it was a shot in the dark)

20 In Scotland in 1546 a Protestant group entered Cardinal Beaton's room to kill him as revenge for Patrick Hamilton's burning. They started to stab him when a priest with them said, 'Stop! Stop! This is not being done God's way.' What did he make them do? (Clue: they can do it with their eyes closed)

Awful Aztecs

In 1519 the Spaniards arrived in Mexico and met the Aztecs. These people made the Tudors look like harmless hamsters. Apart from their horrible habit of human sacrifice, how much do you know about the Aztecs? Answer true or false.

1 Aztec warriors wore metal armour.

2 Aztec princes cut out the hearts of sacrifice victims with a glass knife.

3 Boys were trained to be warriors and were

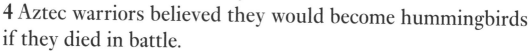

given battle dress when they were still babies.

4 Aztec warriors believed they would become hummingbirds if they died in battle.

5 The Aztecs had public toilets.

6 Warriors with long hair were seen as the best fighters.

7 Aztecs liked to eat scum.

8 An Aztec boy had to ask his best friend for permission to get married.

9 Young Aztec men could be made full warriors by having their faces smeared with the blood of a heart that was still beating.

10 The Spanish caught terrible diseases from the Aztec people.

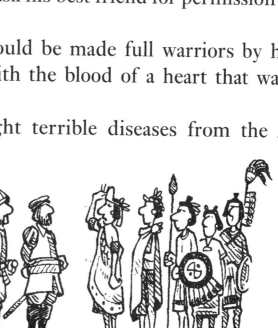

Quick Tudor quiz

1 Margaret's sister died at the same time. It's a fair bet they were both poisoned. James went on to marry Henry VIII's sister instead.

2 Henry VII (who died in 1509) and also his eldest son, Arthur (who died in 1502).

3 He was 70. The oldest Scot in battle, William Maitland, actually fought and died – and he was 90!

4 Catherine sent the bloodstained coat from the dead King of Scotland. Henry was furious. He wanted the glory of the victory for himself. There's no pleasing some people.

5 Patrick Hamilton was burned to death but the damp weather meant he burnt slowly. The executioners tried to put gunpowder on the fire but that only scorched him.

6 Henry ordered that Rosse be boiled alive in his own pot. Rosse always said that he put the poison in the pot as a joke – it wasn't meant to kill.

7 She was hanged along with three men who supported her attack on the king.

8 Very short. He asked the executioner to try and be an accurate shot with the axe.

9 They were all called 'Catherine'.

10 Anne wasn't beheaded on a block. She knelt down and her head was removed with a single swipe of a sword. It was said her lips kept moving in prayer for minutes after her head was off.

11 Henry tried to put it off until he could find an excuse not to do it. He didn't want to marry Anne after all, but he knew if he refused he would upset her powerful father. In the end he had to go ahead.

12 James didn't turn up. James' councillors said Henry was planning a trap.

13 She moved her head around to make the job as difficult as possible for the executioner. It took him several chops at her shoulders before he finally hit her neck and got her head off.

14 Lady Rochford arranged the meetings between Catherine and her boyfriends.

15 Rolled over and sank. It may have been top heavy with guns and men and the boat was upset. Henry was upset too – but 500 people on board were dead upset. Simply dead, in fact.

16 It was illegal for anyone to say, 'The king is going to die.' So they didn't say it – but he died anyway.

17 Henry had died three days earlier on 28 January. The lords wanted his death kept secret for a few days till the throne was safe for Edward VI to take it. They had meals delivered to the room to make it seem normal. But who ate them?

18 She had him burned. Probably not true.

19 The dog was shot dead by the visitor, who was Ed's uncle. He was executed, and the mutt was avenged.

20 Pray. When they finished the prayer they finished off the Bishop. God would be glad about that.

Awful Aztecs

1 False. They had armour but it was made of hardened cotton.

2 True. The knives were made from a type of natural glass called 'obsidian'.

3 True. They were given a loincloth, shield, cloak and four arrows when they were a few days old.

4 True. They believed they would hum off to join the Sun God.

5 True. And the human manure would be used as fertilizer for crops.

6 False. Warriors couldn't get their hair cut until they'd killed someone in battle.

7 True. Lake scum was made into cakes.

8 False. He had to ask his teacher!

9 True.

10 False. The Spanish brought diseases from Europe which killed many Aztecs.

INTERESTING INDEX

Where will you find 'smelly feet', 'fingernails in pies' and 'cut-off ears' in an index? In a Horrible Histories book, of course!

Escape from the terrible Tower

Here's a simple board game for those winter nights. So why not throw another chair on the fire and stretch out in front of its flickering warmth like a prisoner on a rack?

You need a dice and a playing partner. The first to reach the end can have a day off school! (But the day off must be a Sunday.) The loser must suffer the ghastly goat torture (from the Murderous Middle Ages).

13 Lady Jane Grey was executed at the Tower for taking Mary Tudor's throne. How long did Jane hang on to the throne?
a) 9 days
b) 9 weeks

14 A Tower raven dies. Bad luck. Go back to square 9.

15 Walter Raleigh laid his head on the block for the chop and got a message from the king. What did it say?
a) Serves you right
b) Only joking, keep your head on

12 Anne Boleyn's ghost tells you of a secret passage. Crawl forward to square 15.

11 Henry VIII's second wife, Anne Boleyn, was beheaded at the Tower. How?
a) with a slice of a sword
b) with a chop of an axe

10 Henry VIII clears his dungeons by executing all prisoners. Go back to start without your head.

1 Who built the Tower?
a) William the Conqueror
b) William the Torturer

2 A kind jailer's daughter gives you food. Throw dice again.

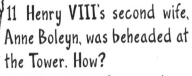

3 Who made Traitor's Gate collapse as it was being built?
a) Thomas a Becket's ghost
b) Viking raiders

START

You start in the Tower of London – one of the most haunted and horrible prisons in history. Take turns rolling the dice and move on the number of spaces shown. If you land on a question and get it right a) award yourself a tasty roast rat from the dungeon and b) throw again, but if you get it wrong a) award youself some water covered in dungeon slime and b) miss a turn. Throw the exact number to finish the game on the 'Freedom' square. Easy!

21 FREEDOM! You are free! Free to go to school. Come to think of it, you were probably better off in the Tower, weren't you?

20 You are on the last step to freedom – but slip on some blood. Tumble back to square 11.

19 The last execution at the Tower was when?
a) 1841
b) 1941

16 You find a diamond from the Crown jewels and bribe a guard. Go to square 19.

17 Colonel Blood stole the Crown Jewels by dressing up to fool the chief guard. He dressed as what?
a) a priest
b) a woman

18 Queen Victoria decides to pardon you as you've been in prison for 300 years. Throw again.

9 Two princes disappeared in 1483 – last seen in the Tower. 150 years later two little bodies were uncovered. Where?
a) in the Tower well
b) under the Tower stairs

8 You are stretched on the rack so thin you can slip through the bars and escape Move on to square 11.

7 What appeared in the Tower in 1303 for the first time?
a) chopping blocks
b) the Crown jewels

4 A dungeon rat chews through your ropes and sets you free. Go to square 7.

5 Welsh Prince Gruffydd died in the Tower. How?
a) he was beheaded with a saw
b) he fell out of a tower trying to escape

6 A fellow prisoner betrays your escape plan and you are locked in chains. Go back to

Quick Questions

Why not pester your parents and find out how much they know about the terrible Tudors with this quick quiz?

1 Henry VII was the first Tudor monarch. He made England wealthy, but the buckles on his wife's shoes were made of what? (Clue: a rare metal for a queen)

2 Henry VII had an unpopular palace pet. It disgraced itself by tearing up his diaries. What sort of pet was this? (Clue: look in a mirror?)

3 In 1487 Henry captured a rebel, Lambert Simnel, and kept him in an unusual place. Where? (Clue: Simnel was a bit of a pudding anyway)

4 In 1488 James III of scotland was wounded in a battle against his son, James IV He asked for a priest to help him. What did the priest help him to do? (Clue: a heavenly job)

5 James IV of Scotland was curious about science. He wanted to experiment with medicine and dentistry himself. He paid a man 70p to let him do what? (Clue: he looked a little down in the mouth)

6 The Tudors said they could trace their family back to the days of an ancient British king who is now famous in a nursery rhyme. Who? (Clue: fiddles)

7 Henry had the simple-minded Duke of Warwick executed in 1499. On his way from his prison cell to the block, what did the daft Duke do? (Clue: no good at geography)

8 Henry had a fortune-teller locked in the tower. What had the man said that upset the king? (Clue: a grave error)

9 In pictures of Henry VII he is never smiling. Why not? (Clue: shy)

JUST A LITTLE OFF THE TOP

10 What happened to Henry VIII's sixth wife, Catherine Parr, who married him in 1543? (Clue a happier fate)

11 Young Edward VI was king but his uncle, Thomas Seymour had been bribing him. With gold? With jewels? No! What could Uncle Tom bribe the King of England with? (Clue: your parents may bribe you with this from time to time!)

12 Edward died in 1553 and the powerful Duke of Northumberland tried to make Lady Jane Grey queen. She lasted nine days until Mary Tudor took her throne. Jane went to the block but had trouble finding it. Why? (Clue: in the dark)

13 Northumberland was also executed. The judges said his heart should be cut from his body. What was the executioner to do with it next? (Clue: bit of a cheek)

14 What happened in 1564 that would affect English lessons in the 21st century? (Clue: a star is born)

15 In 1577 in Oxford, nearly everyone at the law courts died from a contagious disease called typhus. Only a few people survived. Who? (Clue: they escaped with their lives)

16 In 1601 Queen Elizabeth I's favourite, the Earl of Essex, rebelled. He failed and was sentenced to death. How did Liz show mercy to her dear friend? (Clue: quick and clean)

17 Everyone remembers the Spanish armada of 1588. Everyone forgets they came back in 1601. Where did they land? (Clue: sounds like they land on an island?)

18 Just before Elizabeth I died she said she wanted James of Scotland to take her throne. This may have partly made up for what she had done to his mother. What? (Clue: shortened her)

THAT ELIZABETH IS A PAIN IN THE NECK

Painful punishments

What would you do to someone who sold you a theatre ticket … for a play that was never performed? Match these true Tudors crimes and punishments to find out what would have happened in terrible Tudor times…

CRIME	PUNISHMENT
1. Fraud. Richard Vennor sold tickets for a play that never took place.	a) Pressing. Lain on the ground with weights piled on top.
2. Fortune telling. In 1578 sallow Kennth went to Lady Seaforth and told her that her husband was flirting with other women in France.	b) Skeffington's gyves. An iron hoop in two halves joined by a hinge. The prisoner, hands tied behind, knelt in one half while the torturer closed the second half shut. The prisoner was squeezed into a tight ball.
3. Refusing to speak in court. Margaret Clitheroe refused to plead guilty or not–guilty when she was accused of hiding Catholic priests.	c) Thumbscrews. The victim's thumbs were placed under a metal bar. The bar was slowly screwed down so it squeezed the fingernails.
4. Witchcraft. In 1596 Scot Thomas Papley was accused of witchcraft and refused to confess.	d) The hole. Thrown into jail to sleep on bare boards with 50 other prisoners – freezing in winter and suffocating in summer.

5. Spying. England was full of spies from Spain and France who reported back to their masters. It was important to get them to talk before they died.

e) The gauntlets. The prisoner stood on blocks on wood. His (or her) wrists were fastened in iron handcuffs to a beam above their head. One by one the blocks were removed till the prisoner was standing on tiptoe and finally swinging from the beam.

6. Being a Catholic priest. Banned by Elizabeth I. When one was caught he'd be tortured to betray names and hiding places of other Catholics.

f) Whipping stocks. Given twelve strokes on their bare back with a whip with two cords, but without any knots. The victims then were dragged through the streets and locked in the stocks at Cheapside where the crowds could pelt them with rubbish and spit at them.

7. Child cruelty. Eliza Morton was taken in to the poor–house to work because she was a beggar. Then it was discovered she had a child but had left her on the streets in the hope someone would care for her.

THANKS MUM

g) The barrel. Popped into a tar barrel lined with spikes. It was set on fire and rolled down a hill.

WHAT IS IT?

A BURNT ROLL

8. Treason. Prisoners suspected of plotting against the monarch were often tortured so they would name their fellow plotters.

h) The boot. Had a metal boot placed over the foot and wedges driven in till the ankle bones were crushed and splintered.

Fifteen hundreds firsts

Which of these things might you have seen in the 1500s? Answer yes or no…

1. FIREWORKS DISPLAY
2. GUY FAWKES DAY
3. GLASS EYE
4. TOBACCO
5. CIGARETTES
6. THE RUFF
7. POSTAL SERVICE
8. POSTAGE STAMP
9. WRIST WATCH
10. LIPSTICK
11. PENCILS

Medical woes

Tudors weren't just terrible kings and queens. For ordinary people, life was grim. Nine out of ten people never made it to 40!

Read about these four gruesome diseases. Match the description to the putrid pictures below – A, B, C or D – careful you don't catch any nasties from them!

1) SWEATING SICKNESS
Arrived without warning. It caused shivering, sweating and then terrible weakness. If your body stopped sweating, then you started peeing. Many died in the first 24 hours.

2) SMALLPOX
Caused high fever, headaches and muscle pain. Sometimes your lungs filled with blood. If you survived that, a rash appeared and grew into pimples. These burst and the scabs fell off in a few weeks.

3) THE PLAGUE
Started with visibly swollen glands, then fever, chills, headache and extreme exhaustion. If it got into your lungs, you might even cough up blood and die.

4) JAIL FEVER
Caused fever and rashes all over the body. Half of those who caught it died. Caused by head lice (nits) and body lice. They like crowded, dirty conditions– very common in Tudor times!

A
ACHE ACHE

B
ITCH ITCH

C
TINKLE TINKLE

D
DIE DIE

Horrible Henry VIII

You know that Henry VIII had six wives. But did you know that Henry reigned for 38 torturing Tudor years and, in that time, about 72,000 people were executed? That's about 1,900 a year, or five every day. It must have been a bit like a National Lottery with 35 losers every week.

Henry wanted power over everything and everyone – this included the Church. So he got rid of the Catholic Church and made himself head of a Church of England. Henry killed or tortured anyone who opposed it. Here is a list of some of Henry's horrible laws. Work out which ones are TRUE or FALSE and select YEA for yes, NAY for no.

THAT'S WHAT YOU GET WHEN YOU TAKE ON A TUDOR!

TO THE PEOPLE OF ENGLAND

In the name of His Most Royal Majesty, King Henry VIII, defender of the faith, the following laws have been enacted...

1) The king will take the wealth of the monasteries, sell off their lands and close them. — Yea or Nay

2) All monks will worship the king as well as our Lord. — Yea or Nay

3) The Catholic religion will be replaced by the Protestant religion. — Yea or Nay

4) All children must be christened as Protestants. There will be a charge for christenings, marriages and burials. — Yea or Nay

5) Anyone who laughs out loud in front of the king will be hanged. — Yea or Nay

6) Anyone eating white bread must pay a tax to the king. — Yea or Nay

7) When a criminal is hanged his family must pay for the cost of the rope and the hangman. — Yea or Nay

Signed *Thomas Cromwell*

Chief minister

THAT'S NOT FAIR! I'M REVOLTING!

HE ALWAYS HAS BEEN

Bad Queen Bess

Elizabeth I had many plots against her life. She found it hard to trust anyone–even her family. Elizabeth's cousin, Mary Queen of Scots, was Catholic and a lot of English Catholics would like to have seen her on Elizabeth's throne…

Mary Queen of Scots fled from Scotland when her husband was murdered and asked her cousin Elizabeth I to protect her. Elizabeth protected Mary by having her locked away for 19 years. When Mary's Catholic friends became too dangerous then Elizabeth had the Queen of Scots beheaded. End of the Catholic plotters – end of Mary.

Read about Mary's execution, then find the words written in CAPITAL LETTERS in the puzzle. The words are written up, down, diagonally and across.

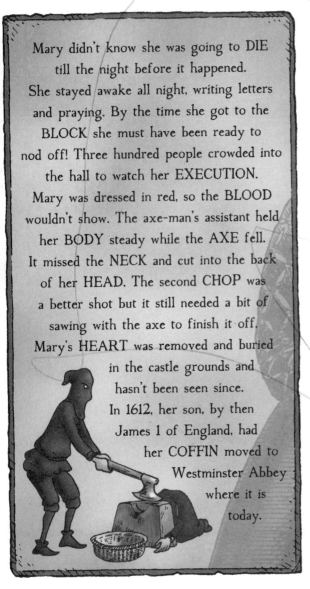

Mary didn't know she was going to DIE till the night before it happened. She stayed awake all night, writing letters and praying. By the time she got to the BLOCK she must have been ready to nod off! Three hundred people crowded into the hall to watch her EXECUTION. Mary was dressed in red, so the BLOOD wouldn't show. The axe-man's assistant held her BODY steady while the AXE fell. It missed the NECK and cut into the back of her HEAD. The second CHOP was a better shot but it still needed a bit of sawing with the axe to finish it off. Mary's HEART was removed and buried in the castle grounds and hasn't been seen since. In 1612, her son, by then James 1 of England, had her COFFIN moved to Westminster Abbey where it is today.

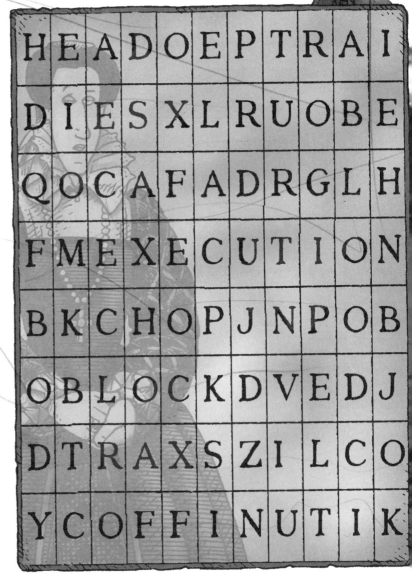

HERE'S SOME MORE COMIN' DOWN JIM!

RIGHTO BOB, I GOT IT! OOH BIG ONE TOO

DID YOU KNOW...?

In Tudor England the great houses and palaces had toilets called 'jakes'. But the waste from the jakes didn't get washed away. It fell down into a pit. With hundreds of people living in a palace these pits soon filled up … and up … and up.

Elizabeth wasn't very popular when she visited other people's houses and filled up their jakes while hers were being emptied. She really was a pain in the bum! Work out which items in this picture you wouldn't see in a Tudor loo.

Shakespearean deaths

Go to Stratford today and you can see lots of murder and violence, torture and execution, suicides and cruelty.

The good news is it is all on stage and the blood is make-believe! Go to a Shakespeare play and there is a good chance you'll see some of the most horrible things ever to appear on a theatre stage.

For a start there are lots of interesting ways to be murdered. Can you guess which unusual way of killing people Shakespeare used in his plays? Clue: only one was a real-life death, but whose...?

1 Cut down in battle and head lopped off

2 Throat cut then baked into a pie and served to his mother

3 Assassinated by twenty-three men with daggers

4 Chased and eaten by a bear[1]

[1]In Shakespeare's day a real bear was borrowed from a bear pit and sent on stage to chase the actor off. He probably wasn't eaten...)

290

5 Poison poured in the ear

6 Stabbed in the eye in a bar brawl

7 Smothered with a pillow

8 Stabbed and body thrown to wild beasts

9 Blown to pieces by a cannonball

10 Buried chest-deep in the earth and left to starve to death

Shakespearean suicides

Shakespeare was not very kind to his characters. He made some so miserable they killed themselves! Can you guess which crazy character matches which disgusting death?

1. Get a poisonous snake to bite you

2. Jump off a castle wall

3. Throw yourself into a river (when you can't swim)

4. Drink poison

5. Stab yourself

6. Get a servant to hold a sword while you run on to it

7. Swallow hot coals

8. Stab yourself with your friend's sword

A. Titinius in *Julius Caesar*
B. Romeo in *Romeo and Juliet*
C. Juliet in *Romeo and Juliet*
D. Cleopatra in *Anthony and Cleopatra*
E. Portia in *Julius Caesar*
F. Lady Macbeth in *Macbeth*
G. Brutus in *Julius Caesar*
H. Ophelia in *Hamlet*

Mary's secret code

When Mary, Queen of Scots, was imprisoned, she used spies to send secret messages. In case they were caught, she used this code to disguise her notes:

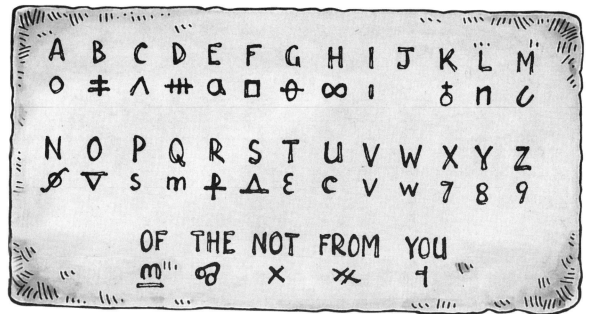

Can you decipher these coded sentences and work out which terrible Tudor monarch they refer to?

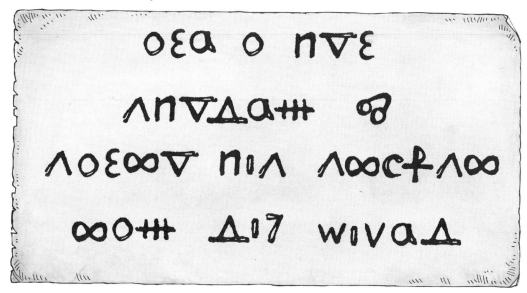

You could try writing your own secret messages in Mary's code. But beware you keep the code secret. Sir Francis Walsingham had a copy of Mary's code and passed it on to Queen Elizabeth. She got hold of Mary's spies and had her beheaded!

Answers

Quick Questions

1   Tin. Henry was rich but extremely mean. His wife had to patch and darn her own dresses.

2   A monkey.

3   He was given a job in Henry's castle kitchen.

4   The priest helped him to die by stabbing him. In fact it wasn't a priest but an enemy lord in disguise. Bad luck, James

5   Take all of his teeth out.

6   Coel Hen Godebog, better known to us has Old King Cole.

7   The Duke almost got lost. He wandered off in the wrong direction. Unfortunately there were guards to lead him to the block.

8   The fortune teller said Henry would be dead before Christmas. He was wrong – and he suffered for it.

9   His teeth were rotten and black.

10 Catherine Parr survived. After Henry VIII died she went on to marry again.

11 Pocket money. It worked for a while but Uncle Tom got power mad and ended up with his neck on the block and his head on the floor.

12 Jane was blindfolded.

13 Throw it in his face! Yeuch!

14 William Shakespeare was born.

15 The prisoners. They were used to filthy conditions and so stood a better chance against the disease.

16 She allowed him to be beheaded without being tortured first.

17 Ireland. They failed to meet up with Irish rebel friends and were defeated.

18 She had James's mother, Mary Queen of Scots, beheaded in 1587.

Painful punishments

1   d) Result – survived.

2   g) Result – death.

3   a) Result – death.

4   h) Result – survived and later executed.

5   b) Result – often death. Leonard Skeffington was in charge of the Tower in the days of Henry VIII. This machine could be carried to the prisoner's

cell and used there, to save trips to the torture chamber.

6   e) Result – usually survived then executed.

7   f) Result – survived.

8   c) Result – survived but hands totally mangled

Fifteen Hundreds Firsts

1   Fireworks display – Yes. 1572, London.

2   Guy Fawkes Day – No. 1607.

3   Glass eye – Yes. 1578, Venice.

4   Tobacco – Yes. First in Europe in 1556.

5   Cigarettes – No. 1843, France.

6   The ruff – Yes. The fashion arrived from France in 1542.

7   Postal service – Yes. Royal Mail set up in 1512.

8   Postage stamp – No. 1653, Paris.

9   Wrist watch – Yes. Elizabeth I had one of the first.

10   Lipstick – No. 1915, though Tudor women did use lip colour.

11   Pencils – Yes. 1584, made of Cumbrian graphite

Medical Woes

1 = C

2 = A

3 = D

4 = B

Horrible Henry VIII

Henry wanted power over everything ... nearly.

1   Yea

2   Nay

3   Yea

4   Yea

5   Nay

6   Yea

7   Nay

Queen Bess Wordsearch

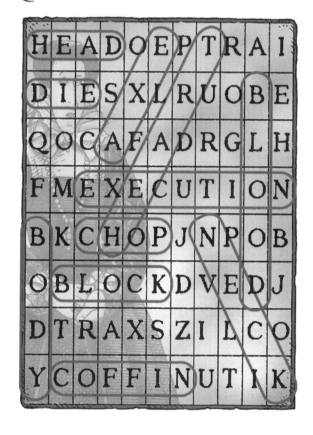

Elizabeth was terrified of being assassinated...

Tudor Toilets

You wouldn't find an air freshener, toilet brush or toilet paper in a Tudor loo. Queen Elizabeth's godson, Sir John Harrington, invented the first flushing toilet. The Queen was so impressed, she had them fitted in all of her palaces

Mary's Secret Code

The Tudor Monarch described is Henry VIII:
1 Ate a lot
2 Closed the Catholic church
3 Had six wives

Shakespearean Death

1 Macbeth in *Macbeth*
2 Chiron in *Titus Andronicus*
3 Julius Caesar in *Julius Caesar*
4 Antigonus in *The Winter's Tale*
5 King Hamlet in *Hamlet*
6 Not in a play! This really happened to Shakespeare's rival playwright, Christopher Marlowe. Or did it...
7 Desdemona in *Othello*
8 Tamora in *Titus Andronicus*
9 Earl Salisbury in *Henry VI*
10 Aaron in *Titus Andronicus*

HORRIBLE HISTORIES

WOEFUL
SECOND WORLD
WAR

TERRY DEARY ILLUSTRATED BY MARTIN BROWN

HORRIBLE HISTORIES

GROOVY
GREEKS

TERRY DEARY ILLUSTRATED BY MARTIN BROWN

HORRIBLE HISTORIES

VILE
VICTORIANS

TERRY DEARY ILLUSTRATED BY MARTIN BROWN

HORRIBLE HISTORIES

FRIGHTFUL
FIRST WORLD
WAR

TERRY DEARY ILLUSTRATED BY MARTIN BROWN

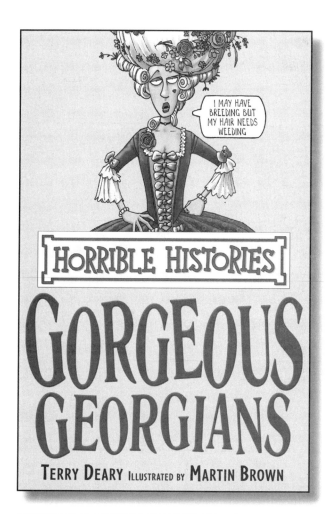

HORRIBLE HISTORIES

GORGEOUS GEORGIANS

I MAY HAVE BREEDING BUT MY HAIR NEEDS WEEDING

TERRY DEARY ILLUSTRATED BY **MARTIN BROWN**

HORRIBLE HISTORIES

SMASHING SAXONS

ALFRED THE GREAT? I'M ALFRED THE BLOOMIN MARVELLOUS

TERRY DEARY ILLUSTRATED BY **MARTIN BROWN**

HORRIBLE HISTORIES

BLITZED BRITS

THE BLITZ IS THE PITS

TERRY DEARY ILLUSTRATED BY **MARTIN BROWN** & **KATE SHEPPARD**

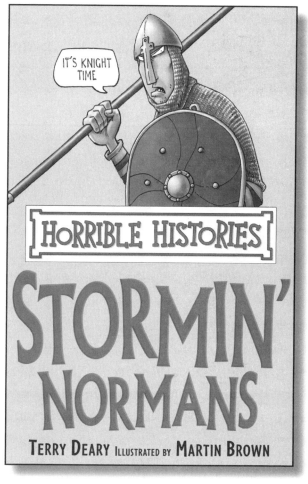

HORRIBLE HISTORIES

STORMIN' NORMANS

IT'S KNIGHT TIME

TERRY DEARY ILLUSTRATED BY **MARTIN BROWN**

HORRIBLE HISTORIES

VICIOUS VIKINGS

TERRY DEARY ILLUSTRATED BY MARTIN BROWN

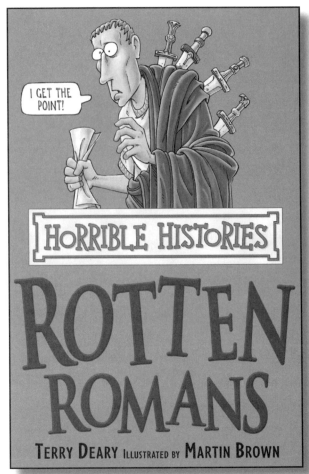

HORRIBLE HISTORIES

ROTTEN ROMANS

TERRY DEARY ILLUSTRATED BY MARTIN BROWN

HORRIBLE HISTORIES

AWESOME EGYPTIANS

TERRY DEARY & PETER HEPPLEWHITE
ILLUSTRATED BY MARTIN BROWN

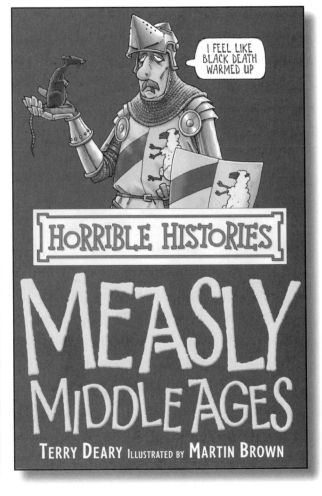

HORRIBLE HISTORIES

MEASLY MIDDLE AGES

TERRY DEARY ILLUSTRATED BY MARTIN BROWN

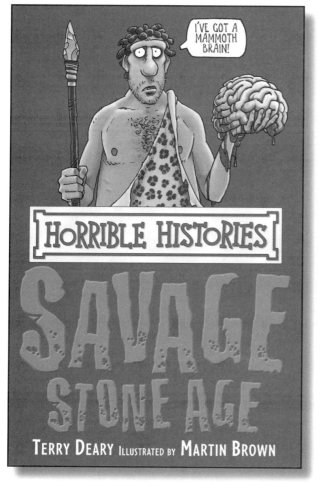

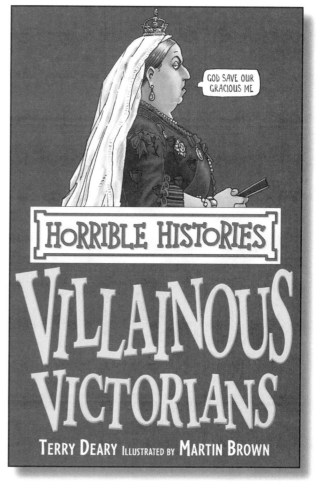

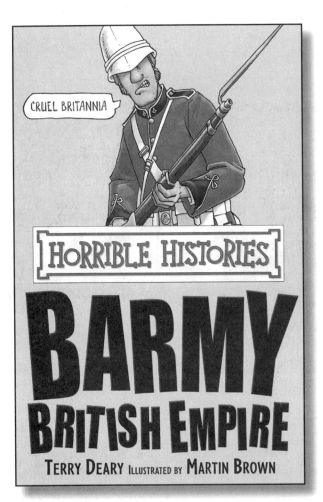

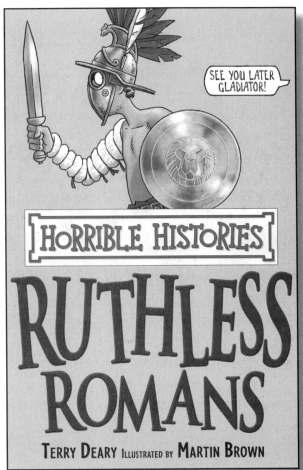

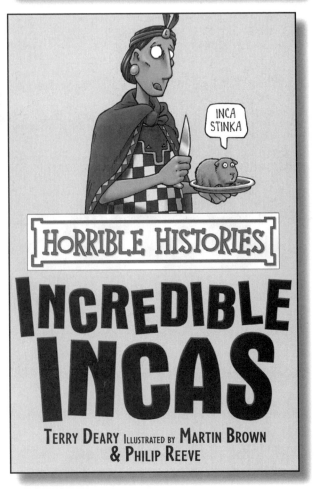

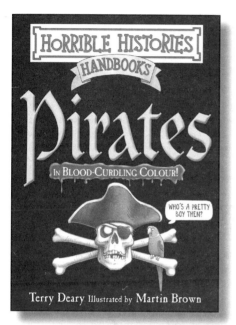

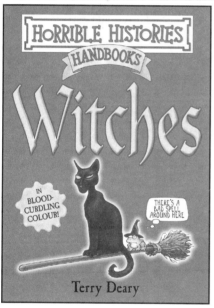

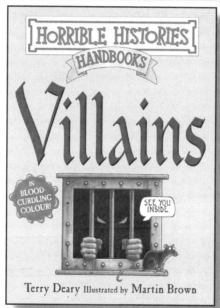

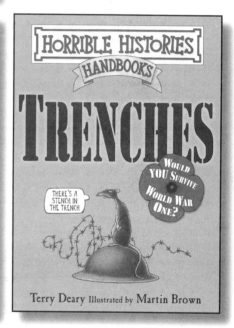

Don't miss these horribly handy handbooks for all the gore and more!

IT'S TOP OF THE POPS!

An Awesome Egyptian Pop-up Adventure!

Three amazing 3D scenes:
Mummy-making mayhem! • Tut's tomb treasure! • Agonizing afterlife!